The Author

DR. GEORGE SWEETING is the president of Moody Bible Institute in Chicago. His wide experience as an evangelist, author, and educator has introduced him to audiences throughout the world. His radio messages over "Moody Presents" are heard weekly by thousands across North and South America and in parts of Europe.

Dr. Sweeting brings to this study of Christian love a pastor's heart, having served several well-known churches, including more than five years as pastor of the historic Moody Memorial Church in Chicago's inner city.

A graduate of Moody Bible Institute, Dr. Sweeting also studied at Gordon College, New York University, and Northern Baptist Seminary. He has been awarded honorary doctorate degrees by Azusa Pacific College, Tennessee Temple University, and Gordon-Conwell Theological Seminary.

He is the author of numerous books, including *How to Solve Conflicts* and *The City: A Matter of Conscience.*

Love Is the Greatest

Love Is the Greatest

by

GEORGE SWEETING

MOODY PRESS

CHICAGO

Revised Edition, © 1974 by
THE MOODY BIBLE INSTITUTE
OF CHICAGO

Original Title: *And the Greatest of These*
© 1968 by George Sweeting

Third Printing, 1975

ISBN: 0-8024-5022-9

All scripture quotations in this book are taken from *The New Scofield Reference Edition of the Holy Bible* (New York: Oxford, 1967), except where indicated otherwise. Used by permission.

The use of selected references from various versions of the Bible in this publication does not necessarily imply publisher endorsement of the versions in their entirety.

Printed in the United States of America

To my loving wife,
HILDA MARGRET SWEETING,
whose life and patience have been a
source of constant inspiration to me

CONTENTS

1 CORINTHIANS 13

1. Though I speak with the tongues of men and of angels, and have not charity, I am become as sounding brass, or a tinkling cymbal.

2. And though I have the gift of prophecy, and understand all mysteries, and all knowledge; and though I have all faith, so that I could remove mountains, and have not charity, I am nothing.

3. And though I bestow all my goods to feed the poor, and though I give my body to be burned, and have not charity, it profiteth me nothing.

4. Charity suffereth long, and is kind; charity envieth not; charity vaunteth not itself, is not puffed up.

5. Doth not behave itself unseemingly, seeketh not her own, is not easily provoked, thinketh no evil;

6. Rejoiceth not in iniquity, but rejoiceth in the truth;

7. Beareth all things, believeth all things, hopeth all things, endureth all things.

8. Charity never faileth: but whether there be prophecies, they shall fail; whether there be tongues, they shall cease; whether there be knowledge, it shall vanish away.

9. For we know in part, and we prophesy in part.

10. But when that which is perfect is come, then that which is in part shall be done away.

11. When I was a child, I spake as a child, I understood as a child, I thought as a child: but when I became a man, I put away childish things.

12. For now we see through a glass, darkly; but then face to face: now I know in part; but then shall I know even as also I am known.

13. And now abideth faith, hope, charity, these three; but the greatest of these is charity.

The King James Version of the Holy Bible

1

THE SEARCH FOR LOVE

"With loving-kindness have I drawn thee" (Jeremiah 31:3).

Our world is starving for love. Deep down inside every human being, God has planted a thirst for Himself that is never satisfied until we are united with Him.

> There is a God-shaped vacuum in every heart.
>
> BLAISE PASCAL

As I sit here writing at my desk in Chicago, this city of four million people is literally paralyzed under two feet of snow. Beyond my frozen windows the broad streets and expressways, usually jammed with traffic, are deserted—transformed by windblown drifts into long, unbroken sweeps of white snow.

Here and there, as snow fell steadily during the day, I could see a modern pioneer venturing beyond his own front door. In the warm security of my study, I found myself wondering what had motivated him to slowly, tediously shovel his way outdoors: the spirit of adventure? the instinct of self-preservation? love for people?

THE PROBLEM OF MANKIND

Night is falling now, and the more vigorous people have struggled free of the storm's grip. "Hello, there! How are you doing?" rings across the street between neighbors who heretofore have scarcely spoken. A blizzard has a unique way of transforming big-city impersonality into small-town friendliness. My favorite radio newscaster, reporting on the storm,

9

commented on this and added that this sort of mass emergency always brings out both the *best* and the *beast* in human beings. The day's news items soon confirmed this. In one end of the city an impromptu chain of command grew into a neighborhood crew of one hundred fifty people, shoveling in teams of three, to release their families from the blizzard's clutch.

An energetic gang of high-school boys worked under police supervision, digging out seventy-five buried automobiles and hauling several ill persons by toboggan to waiting ambulances. Twenty-five girls in the same suburb did volunteer duty in two hospitals to replace regular staff members who were snowbound in their homes.

However, at the same time, elsewhere in Chicago, a truck driver was held captive in the cab of his own stalled truck while a crowd robbed him of his cargo—twenty thousand pounds of meat. A group of youths and housewives looted a stalled soft drink truck of two hundred cases of beverages, which they dragged by sled to their homes.

> A man who is at war with himself will be at war with others.
>
> DAG HAMMERSKJOLD

> All my life I have been seeking to climb out of the pit of my besetting sins and I cannot do it and I never will unless a hand is let down to draw me up.
>
> SENECA

This constant conflict between good and evil, between love and hate has tragically crippled mankind since human history began. Man has an astounding capacity for both selfishness and kindness, for both hate and love. When forced into a situation that threatens him, he will frighten even himself by his ability to cheat, steal, lie, and hate. But his happiest moments come, quite unexpectedly, when he finds himself spontaneously giving or doing something to help someone else.

We can all remember the warm feeling of such moments: the

annual glow that settles briefly over the world at Christmastime, the surge of caring that lifts up the bereaved when death has struck, the thoughtfulness of a housewife who does an invalid neighbor's marketing along with her own. We are touched when we see our elder child help a younger sister with her homework, or see our youngest child reach out in unexpected sympathy and love to comfort a hurt playmate.

We feel a little better about the younger generation when we watch the boys next door put up the storm windows for the widow across the way; a little better about adults when our neighborhood chips in to buy a wheelchair for someone in need, or the family down the road opens its arms to an unhappy deserted foster child. All of us have experienced the surge of deep satisfaction that fills our hearts when we break free of our own selfishness to share our love with others in need.

> Because God cares, we care. Because He loves us, wretched as we are, we must love others, wretched as they are.

And all of us know, too, the sad moments of shame we feel because we do this so rarely. "For that which I do I understand not," wrote the apostle Paul, "for what I would, that do I not; but what I hate, that do I. . . . I find then a law, that, when I would do good, evil is present with me" (Romans 7.15, 21). No single factor has so limited the Christian church down through the years as man's inhumanity to man—sometimes outright cruelty, but far more often, sheer lovelessness. There is no doubt about it: our world is restless and starving for God's love.

> Thou hast made us for thyself, and the heart of man is restless until it finds its rest in Thee.
>
> AUGUSTINE

This matter of getting along with people has become such a staggering problem to psychologists that our century is sometimes called "the age of human relations." Our relationships with others often become incredibly unmanageable. But we will never consistently improve them until Jesus Christ rearranges us away from self and toward God and our fellow man.

There is a very good reason for the order in which Christ stated His two great commandments—the second commandment being absolutely impossible without the first! Love of neighbor can only become a reality for us as we love the Lord our God with all our hearts, souls, and minds.

DOES ANYONE CARE?

> I feel the capacity to care is the thing which gives life
> its deepest significance.
>
> PABLO CASALS

I was shaken by a small newspaper item recently about a fourteen-year-old boy who took his own life because "no one seemed to care." He had felt no sense of love from anyone except his dog, and in a brief suicide note addressed to his parents he left instructions for the dog's care.

No one seemed to care. What a stark summation of our world's lack of love—or lack of sharing and showing it. Quite likely that boy's parents really did love him, but they evidently failed to let him know it, and his suicide illustrated sharply how minor deeds of lovelessness add up to major tragedies. This boy was searching for love, and he didn't find it.

The origin of the word "sympathy" implies to suffer with. It means "to weep with those who weep." It is a silent kind of deep understanding love when heart meets heart.

> We share our mutual woes, our mutual burdens bear;
> And often for each other flows, the sympathizing tear.
>
> FREDERICK W. FABER

Gypsy Smith used to tell how one of his sons came to his study one day when he was very busy. Gypsy offered the boy the use of a special knife, but the boy rejected it. He tried to interest his son in a number of things but had no success. Finally he asked, "Son, what in the world do you want?" The boy replied sadly, "Daddy, I just want you."

> Love does not die easily. It is a living thing. It thrives in the face of all life's hazards, save one—neglect.
>
> JAMES D. BRYDEN

This is not particularly a revolutionary statement of new truth; it is the heartbreaking experience that we have day after day. Frustration, loneliness, self-pity, indifference, emptiness, hostility, hatred, closeheartedness, resentment, jealousy, and the resultant criminal acts, all grow like wild weeds to fill the holes gouged in our hearts when nobody seems to care.

> Persons are to be loved; things are to be used.
>
> REUEL HOWE

People of all ages and cultures have a sensitivity to real love; and when God's love comes through with unmistakable clarity, an amazing, mysterious energy leaps forth in response. And God, who is love, once again is revealed through the act of people loving each other.

> What one single ability do we all have?
> The ability to change.
>
> L. ANDREWS

> That sense of newness is simply delicious. It makes new the Bible, and friends, and all mankind, and love, and spiritual things, and Sunday, and church and God Himself. So I've found.
>
> TEMPLE GARDNER OF CAIRO

The good news of the gospel is that change is possible for each one. One of the reasons for Christ's not remaining on earth in human form was that more power would be available to all men through the gift of the Holy Spirit. Jesus told His disciples, "The Comforter, who is the Holy Spirit, whom the

Father will send in my name . . . shall teach you all things, and
bring all things to your remembrance, whatever I have said
unto you" (John 14:26). "But ye shall receive power, after
the Holy Spirit is come upon you" (Acts 1:8). Yes, we desperately need God's power to live and to love.

> We ourselves were sure that at long last a generation
> had arisen keen and eager, to put this disorderly
> earth to right . . . and fit to do it . . . we meant so
> well, we tried so hard, and look what we have made
> of it. We can only muddle in the muddle. What is
> required is a new kind of man.
>
> WALTER LIPPMAN

MY SEARCH FOR LOVE

To the Christian, whose whole life has come alive with God's
Spirit, there is nothing more important in all this world than
learning how to love.

Do you know how to love? Do you remember the story of
Jesus and the rich young man? The youth had obeyed all the
commandments of his Jewish tradition, but when Jesus told
him to give his money to the poor—a supreme test of love in
his case—he turned away sadly. He came to the right person,
asked the right question, heard the right answer, but made the
wrong decision. He went away sad.

The disciples who had overheard the conversation were
shocked. "Who, then, can be saved?" they asked. And Jesus
looked at them intently. "With men this is impossible, but with
God all things are possible" (Matthew 19:25-26). The Bible
is very clear on the point that if we have money enough to live
well, and don't share it with others in need, it is questionable
whether God's love is in us at all.

> All the beautiful sentiments in the world weigh less
> than a single lovely action.
>
> J. LOWELL

"My little children, let us not love in word, neither in tongue, but in deed and in truth" (1 John 3:18). Real love is always giving, and the gift is the love of the giver, God Himself.

MY AWAKENING TO LOVE

A variety of personal experiences in my life alerted me to the supreme calling of love. The earliest occurred when I was a student at Moody Bible Institute. An illness led to an operation which disclosed a serious tumor. My bed in Chicago's Swedish Covenant Hospital became my altar as I dedicated myself anew to God's service. During the course of the ensuing thirty radium treatments, I was told I possibly would not live long, and that even if I did, it was unlikely I would ever be able to have children.

That experience, along with the reading of a pamphlet by James McConkey on God's love, prepared me to become a living sacrifice. That was over thirty years ago, and I am not only still here and apparently healthy, but I have fathered four sons. Over the years I have, at weaker moments, tried to climb down from that altar, but God in His grace has kept me there.

> Love so amazing, so divine, demands my soul, my life, my all.
>
> ISAAC WATTS

Some time later I was speaking in a church in Michigan, where I had been invited for a seven-day series of meetings. After the service one morning, I was painfully aware that I was failing. There seemed to be little explanation for it, but nothing had gone right. After the people had left the church, I stayed behind and knelt at the front pew. I prayed, I wept and my heart was broken before God. The Lord made me painfully aware of my dishonest old self, and of my own personal, selfish ambitions. I told the Lord that I needed help—His help—right away.

That morning, as I poured out my soul in confession, I made

up my mind to pray daily for the gift of love. I vowed not to let anything hinder the development of this grace within. I asked the Lord to help me follow after love, to make the love of Christ the very foundation of my entire life. The difference in my life since that day has been revolutionary. Love has become my dynamic purpose! And today, more than ever before, I am convinced that Christ's love shining through us, working through us, is the only answer to the conflicts of our chaotic world.

The purpose of this book is to encourage you and help you to make God's love the aim of your life. Examine with me the nature of God's love, and our human reflection of God's love to other people. Learn with me how to love. Together, let us discover how to lay hold of the power of God that makes loving possible and even spontaneous.

REMINDERS

- "My little children, let us not love in word, neither in tongue; but in deed and in truth" (1 John 3:18).

- Our world is literally starving for love, God's love.

- No single factor has so limited the Christian church down through the years as man's inhumanity to man—sometimes outright cruelty, but far more often, sheer lovelessness.

- A man who is at war with himself will be at war with others. DAG HAMMARSKJOLD

- Frustration, loneliness, self-pity, indifference, emptiness, hostility, hatred, closeheartedness, resentment, jealousy, and the resultant criminal acts, all grow like wild weeds to fill the holes gouged in our hearts when nobody seems to care.

- The Bible is very clear on the point that if we have money enough to live well, and do not share with others in need, it is questionable whether God's love is in us at all.

- Real love is always giving, and the gift is the love of the giver, God Himself.

1 CORINTHIANS 13

Love gives quality to all other gifts

$^{12:31}$ And yet I will show you a way that is better by far:
If I could speak the languages of men, of angels too,
And have no love,
I am only a rattling pan or a clashing cymbal.
^{2} If I should have the gift of prophecy,
And know all secret truths, and knowledge in its every form,
And have such perfect faith that I could move mountains,
But have no love, I am nothing.
^{3} If I should dole out everything I have for charity,
And give my body up to torture in mere boasting pride;
But have no love, I get from it no good at all.
^{4} Love is so patient and so kind;
Love never boils with jealousy;
It never boasts, is never puffed with pride;
^{5} It does not act with rudeness, or insist upon its rights;
It never gets provoked, it never harbors evil thoughts;
^{6} Is never glad when wrong is done,
But always glad when truth prevails;
^{7} It bears up under anything,
It exercises faith in everything,
It keeps up hope in everything,
It gives us power to endure in anything.
^{8} Love never fails;
If there are prophecies, they will be set aside;
If now exist ecstatic speakings, they will cease;
If there is knowledge, it will soon be set aside;
^{9} For what we know is incomplete and what we prophesy is
incomplete.
^{10} But when perfection comes, what is imperfect will be set aside.
^{11} When I was a child, I talked like a child,
I thought like a child, I reasoned like a child.
When I became a man, I laid aside my childish ways.
^{12} For now we see a dim reflection in a looking-glass,
But then I shall know perfectly, as God knows me.
Now what I know is imperfect,
But them I shall know perfectly, as God knows me.
^{13} And so these three, faith, hope, and love endure,
But the greatest of them is love.

The New Testament in the Language of the People by Charles B. Williams (Chicago: Moody, 1972). Used by permission of Edith S. Williams.

2

MAKE LOVE YOUR AIM

"Follow after love" (1 Corinthians 14:1).

Goals are important!

All the activities of life—from the corporate board room to the baseball diamond—are centered around definite goals. The businessman's goal is to serve people and to increase profits, the ball player wants to reach home plate, and everyone else is motivated, to one degree or another, to achieve certain measurable goals.

> There is no more miserable human being than one in whom nothing is habitual but indecision.
>
> W. JAMES

When all is said and done, the accomplishment of any goal, whatever it is, requires at least two things: discipline and determination. Some one has given us this brief suggestion for achievement: "Plan more work than you can do, then do it. Bite off more than you can chew, then chew it. Hitch your wagon to a star, hold your seat and there you are."

Goals are helpful.

MAKE LOVE YOUR GOAL

> When you have to make a choice and don't make it, that is in itself a choice.
>
> W. JAMES

In 1 Corinthians 14:1 the apostle urges every Christian to make love the supreme goal of his life. "Follow after love,"

19

writes Paul. The word "follow" is a strenuous word. It is the same word used to describe Paul's fierce pursuit and persecution of the early Christians prior to his conversion. This same word is used by Paul when he speaks of pressing, "toward the mark for the prize of the high calling of God in Christ Jesus" (Philippians 3:14).

> When God wanted sponges and oysters He made them and put one on a rock and the other in the mud. When He made man he did not make him to be a sponge or an oyster; He made him with feet and hands, and head and heart, and vital blood, and a place to use them and He said to him, "Go work."
> HENRY WARD BEECHER

Love is work. It demands both conscious and unconscious effort. It demands a continuous, twenty-four-hour-a-day commitment.

> They are decided only to be undecided, resolved to be irresolute, adamant for drift, all-powerful for impotence.
> W. CHURCHILL

Even the nicest, friendliest person becomes hard to love sooner or later. Just about the time you think you really love someone, you discover in an outbreak of hostility that you still have a long, long way to go.

Whether it is your child who has just spilled ink all over your best chair, or your mother-in-law who forgot to remind you of a phone call, you learn that natural love does wear thin. Human love simply is not enough to cope with the pressures of daily living.

When your two-year-old is nodding in his high chair, your warm feeling of love nearly melts your buttons. But when he climbs down from his chair and begins writing on the wall, you know you need special help, if that warm feeling is to keep from exploding.

Perhaps you have no family, and your life moves matter-of-factly from one day to the next. You really are never tested in your ability to love because you are not close to anyone. Then one day something happens—you realize you are out of touch with people and all alone. You have no one to love, no one who cares much about you. You find that you really do not know how to love. Maybe you are not even sure what love is. Perhaps a college romance once shattered your dreams, and you decided that you would not get hurt again. Love for you is nothing more than an empty word. But may I challenge you again to "follow after love."

> A man with a half volition goes backwards and forwards, and makes no way on the smoothest road; a man with a whole volition advances on the roughest, and will reach his purpose, if there be even a little worthiness in it. The man without a purpose is like a ship without a rudder—a waif, a nothing, a no man. Have a purpose in life and having it, throw such strength of mind and muscle into your work as God has given you."
>
> THOMAS CARLYLE

WHAT IS LOVE

The word "love" is tossed about very carelessly. It is used to describe a multitude of things. You may just love pancakes; your son may love to ski; the girl next door may be head over heels in love with your son; you may sing solemnly in church about "Love divine, all loves excelling;" your community may express its love to a destitute family by collecting food and clothing.

Our English language is very limited when it comes to defining love. We use the same word to describe romance, affection, compassion, and enjoyment; as well as to describe our relationship to Almighty God. In reality, true love defies description. There is no neat little definition that encompasses all the avenues love may take. And because love cannot be packaged or bottled, many people today are pursuing a myth— they are frantically trying to discover a love that may not even exist. For these, love is nothing more than a fictitious dream.

While for many people love is only an illusion, the Bible deals in realities. The Word of God gives us some insight into the true meaning of love. It is this biblical definition of love that I will be using throughout this book. Love is that divine force that draws a man to God and to men and women who are made in the image of God. And we can only know this wonderful love as we know God; there is no other way.

> Love is exclusively a Person.
> NORMAN GRUBB

God is love. And the only reason for our human existence is to contain Him, to be channels of His love. Many times the Bible calls us vessels. A vessel is a hollow object made to hold something; God has made human beings to be His vessels, and He expects us to contain Him.

A vessel is useless if it remains empty. But it is also useless if it contains the wrong substance. A basket that is full of apples cannot be filled with oranges. The vessels of our lives can never contain the love of God until first they are emptied of all other contents.

If our whole purpose in life is to contain Jesus Christ, to be filled with His love, then we are wise to get on with the supreme business for which we were created. Making Christ's love the aim of our life is the work of every individual, whether a grandmother, a tool and die maker, a coed, or a defense attorney.

> Apart from blunt truth, our lives sink decadently
> amid the perfume of hints and suggestions.
> A. N. WHITEHEAD

None of us had anything to do with being born into this world, yet we are here. We all possess this thing called life, and we must each determine what we will do with it. Our time on earth is extremely short. Life is pictured in the Bible as a falling leaf, a fading flower, a darting shadow, a flying arrow, a pursuing eagle, a moving shuttle, a vanishing vapor. We are here one moment and gone the next. Our earthly life is so short that the wood of the cradle rubs up tightly against the marble of the tomb. So let's make sure that we fulfill God's purpose for the living. Make love your aim.

LOVE IS SUPREME

It is impossible to read all the books, see all the sights, hear all the people, and experience all the possibilities of life. Our real problem in life is that of selection. It is the problem of priorities that faces each of us. We must choose the very best, we must go after the greatest good. Let us always remember that love is supreme.

> The quality, not the longevity, of one's life is what is important.
> MARTIN LUTHER KING, JR.

One of the little plaques that I keep on my desk reads, "Keep off the detours." Too many people today are wandering all over the place. They are constantly searching for fulfillment but never zeroing in on the work God has for them. We need to stay on the mark! May each one of us resolve to permit nothing to deflect the magnetic needle of our calling—follow after love.

The apostle Paul, in writing to the church at Corinth, listed many interesting gifts, but he concludes that the way of love is "a more excellent way" (1 Corinthians 12:31). He plainly announces that God's love is better and greater than any other possible gift. The scholar Beets renders this phrase, "a surpassingly good way I show you." Lias translates it, "I show you an eminently excellent way." The apostle is simply saying, "Love is the greatest."

Not only did Paul place divine love as supreme, Peter came

to the same conclusion: He taught the early church many things, but he too rated love as the very best way of life. "And above all things," said Peter, "have fervent love among yourselves; for love shall cover the multitude of sins" (1 Peter 4:8). Peter encouraged them above all to give themselves to love. We may fall short and fail in other areas of our lives, but let us make sure we are right in experiencing and reflecting God's love.

Tradition tells us about the aged apostle John, saying farewell to his congregation. When the members asked him for a parting message, John answered by encouraging them to love one another. "Oh," they said, "we've heard that before. Give us something different. Give us a new commandment." He paused for a moment and then said, "A new commandment I give unto you, that ye love one another" (Jn 13:34). John had nothing else to say; everything was wrapped up in one big bundle of love for God, love for God's people, and love for a needy world.

> It is our care for the helpless, our practice of loving kindness, that brands us in the eyes of many of our opponents. "Look!" they say. "How they love one another! Look how they are prepared to die for one another."
>
> TERTULLIAN

Many of the early Christians followed the practice of setting aside a room in their homes to be reserved for people in need. They called these special rooms, "Christ rooms." This extension of God's love to other people in the form of hospitality was accepted in that day as a serious responsibility. Those early Christians teach us, who are surrounded by today's modern paganism, an important lesson: It was their style of living that convinced their neighbors in those Greek and Roman cities of the reality of Jesus Christ. Some superpower was in them. They were vessels filled with the unusual love of Jesus Christ the Son of God.

Do your neighbors see the love of Jesus in you? Sometimes it is much easier to tell people about Christ's love than it is to demonstrate that love in our lives. Dr. Will Houghton, former president of Moody Bible Institute, expressed his desire to be God's vessel in these words:

> Love this world through me, Lord
> This world of broken men,
> Thou didst love through death, Lord
> Oh, love in me again!
> Souls are in despair, Lord.
> Oh, make me know and care;
> When my life they see,
> May they behold Thee,
> Oh, love the world through me.

Yes, that expresses the cry of my life, too.

Long ago a Pharisee questioned the Saviour: "Master, which is the great commandment in the law?" Jesus answered him, "Thou shalt love the Lord, thy God, with all thy heart, and with all thy soul, and with all thy mind. . . . Thou shalt love thy neighbor as thyself" (Matthew 22:36-37, 39).

It is not possible to really love God and hate or wrongfully treat people. "Love worketh no ill to its neighbor," wrote Paul to the church at Rome, "therefore love is the fulfilling of the law" (Romans 13:10).

In an article entitled, "Love—The Way to Spiritual Maturity," Ray Anderson suggests that, "It is possible to have compassion without love, and it is possible to have kindness without love; but it is impossible for one who has put on love to be unkind and without compassion, for love itself is not just an accessory garment. Love is the complete garment that has all the others built into it, so that love is a total way of life."

I once heard of an artist who was commissioned to design a trademark. After some time he submitted his design and a bill for one thousand dollars. The design was unusually simple, and the client questioned the artist on the steep price. "The charge is for knowing what to leave out," answered the artist. In the business of living, it is important that we know what to leave out. There are so many things that detract us, that use up our time and energies. We must learn to leave out the trivialities and concentrate on the essentials. Decide right now to "follow after love."

In his booklet entitled, "The Tyranny of the Urgent" Charles E. Hummel writes, "Our greatest danger in life, is in permitting the urgent things to crowd out the important." Pursuing God's love rarely seems urgent to us—but, my friend, it is desperately important!

> The man who has not learned to say no will be weak
> if not a wretched man as long as he lives.
>
> ALEXANDER MACLAREN

God's love is the lubricating oil for the frictions of life. Love can win over lawlessnes. Love is the only cure for hate. Love is color blind to skin. Love is God's healing medicine for the individual soul as well as for the world. Love is God's answer to man's questions. Love is the supreme ingredient of life!

THREE WORDS FOR LOVE

The Greek language has words for three different dimensions of love. The first word is *eros,* meaning a self-gratifying love. It is not found anywhere in the Bible. This is a physical expression of love, passion seeking satisfaction. Although it is pleasurable, it is self-centered and short-lived.

Eros is the word used in pagan writings to describe the love of one sex toward the other. C. S. Lewis says that eros is "that kind of love which lovers are in." Eros—ask any schoolgirl— is strong, sweet, and terrifying! It needs help, or it either dies or becomes a demon.

The second word is *philia,* or companionate love. This is the love which exists between good friends or between parents and children. It speaks of affection, fondness, or liking. The name Philadelphia comes from this root word and means, "city of brotherly love." Our word, philanthropy, also has its source in "philia" meaning "love of man."

> Infantile love follows the principle: "I love because I am loved." Mature love follows the principle: "I am loved because I love." Immature love says: "I love you because I need you." Mature love says: "I need you because I love you."
>
> ERICH FROMM

Dr. Kenneth S. Wuest described philia as that "love called out of one's heart by the pleasure one takes in the object loved." We feel this kind of love for people with whom we are familiar. We do not always know when affection begins; often we discover only after someone has gone, how fond we were of him.

By itself, philia is a quiet, comfortable feeling for people we usually take for granted. Much of the solid, genuine happiness of our lives comes from our humble affections for each other. But philia, too, needs divine help.

The third word used for love is *agape*, an unselfish, sacrificial love. Again Wuest suggests that this is "a love called out of one's heart by the preciousness of the object loved. It is a love of esteem, of evaluation. It has the idea of prizing. It is . . . the noblest word for love in the Greek language."

> Yes, love is the magic key of life—not to get what we want but to become what we ought to be.
>
> EILEEN GUDER

This word speaks of God's love for us and in us. The word is seldom found in classical Greek, as the pagan world was unaware of its power or reality. The foundation of this love is God Himself, and we see this love demonstrated at Bethlehem's manger and Calvary's cross. This is the love we desperately need in order to make sense out of the others; this is the love that brings stature and glory to eros and philia.

W. E. Vine describes agape as "the chief characteristic word of Christianity." It is the foundation stone of any life in Christ. Without God's help, our other loves cannot even remain what they start out to be, or become what they promise. Only as God's love pours into us can any other love receive a firm foundation.

> Only the loving will have any understanding of love—just as only the good will understand goodness. When one has gotten only a little way into loving, one learns that what understanding we do attain, poor and partial as it must be, is not gotten by thinking about it. It comes by receiving and giving love, as a part of the process of living.
>
> EILEEN GUDER

Some time ago a woman told me that all her life she had been hungry for love. As a child she would do anything to win approval from her friends and family. She always wanted her mother to hug her and her father to buy her expensive gifts as tokens of their love.

Immediately upon her graduation from high school she married, but her relationship with her husband never progressed beyond the physical level. She knew she still had not found any satisfying love. Having one baby after another, she began living for her four children. The torment was tearing her up inside, and nothing seemed to help.

Then one day a neighbor invited her to a Bible class in her home, and she heard the good news that Jesus Christ loved her. Suddenly she sensed that here was the love she had been looking for all her life—here was Someone who loved and accepted her just as she was. She eagerly invited Christ into her life and began at last to come alive.

Despite the joy of her newfound love, this woman was still overwhelmed by the gulf that remained between her husband and God. Then one day her friend suggested that she should demonstrate the love of Christ to her husband right in her own home. She began to really work at loving her family. Gradually she realized how many things needed changing in her life. There was her loud, nagging voice—the Spirit of God taught her how to hold her tongue. Her housekeeping improved. Even her meals showed more love and originality. She worked off excess pounds. Instead of going back to bed after her husband left for work, she stayed up and enjoyed breakfast with the children, and had prayer and Bible reading with them before they left for school.

As God's love kept softening and changing her, the woman's love for her husband and children expressed itself in dozens of ways that softened her family too! One day her husband went out the door and then turned around and came back. He took her in his arms and kissed her good-bye—something he had not done in years.

And what a thrill as she tucked her five-year-old into bed to hear her say, "Mommy, it's so nice since we started loving Jesus, isn't it?"

Only in Jesus' name can our human love blossom forth in beauty and power! Have you ever experienced the transforming power of God's love in your life? Have you ever felt the warmth of God's love expressed in His Son Jesus Christ? God's love can change your life. It is the apex of all grace, the zenith of all gifts. It can give you a reason for living. It can put a smile on your face, a song on your lips, and God's peace deep down in your heart!

Follow after love. Make love your aim. Be a one-eyed person. That is what Jesus was saying when He said, "If, therefore, thine eye be healthy, thy whole body shall be full of light" (Matthew 6:22). Be jealous of anything that would detract or hinder you in your pursuit of this gift, and remember—love is the greatest!

SUGGESTED PRAYER

Heavenly Father! I admit my need of love. I see the gift of love as the excellent way. Thy love is like heavenly oil to overcome the frictions of life. Thy love is the cure for hate and the remedy for lawlessness. Thy love is color blind to skin. Today I would vow a vow to follow after love. May I guard against all that would hinder me in this daily pursuit. Let nothing detract me from this surpassingly good way. Help me, heavenly Father, to follow after love. Amen.

REMINDERS

- "Follow after love" (1 Corinthians 14:1).
- Love is work. It demands both conscious and unconscious effort.
- "Love is exclusively a Person." NORMAN GRUBB
- "Keep off the detours."
- "Our greatest danger in life, is in permitting the urgent things to crowd out the important." CHARLES E. HUMMEL
- Without God's help, our other loves cannot even remain what they start out to be, or become what they promise.

1 CORINTHIANS 13

1. If I speak with the tongues of men and of angels, but do not have love, I have become a noisy gong or a clanging cymbal.

2. And if I have the gift of prophecy, and know all mysteries and all knowledge; and if I have all faith, so as to remove mountains, but do not have love, I am nothing.

3. And if I give all my possessions to feed the poor, and if I deliver my body to be burned, but do not have love, it profits me nothing.

4. Love is patient, love is kind, and is not jealous; love does not brag and is not arrogant,

5. does not act unbecomingly; it does not seek its own, is not provoked, does not take into account a wrong suffered,

6. does not rejoice in unrighteousness, but rejoices with the truth;

7. bears all things, believes all things, hopes all things, endures all things.

8. Love never fails; but if there are gifts of prophecy, they will be done away; if there are tongues, they will cease; if there is knowledge, it will be done away.

9. For we know in part, and we prophesy in part;

10. but when the perfect comes, the partial will be done away.

11. When I was a child, I used to speak as a child, think as a child, reason as a child; when I became a man, I did away with childish things.

12. For now we see in a mirror dimly, but then face to face; now I know in part, but then I shall know fully just as I also have been fully known.

13. But now abide faith, hope, love, these three; but the greatest of these is love.

The New American Standard Version of the Bible (Chicago: Moody, 1973). Copyright 1960, 1962, 1963, 1971, 1973 by the Lockman Foundation. Used by permission.

3

LOVE IS THE GREATEST

"Though I speak with the tongues of men and of angels, and have not love, I am become as sounding brass, or a tinkling cymbal. And though I have the gift of prophecy, and understand all mysteries, and all knowledge; and though I have all faith, so that I could remove mountains, and have not love, I am nothing. And though I bestow all my goods to feed the poor, and though I give my body to be burned, and have not love, it profiteth me nothing" (vv. 1-3).

In January 1956, *Life* Magazine told of the shocking death of five young missionaries in the jungles of Ecuador. For several months these men had tried to make contact with the primitive Auca Indians. On their first successful attempt at communicating the gospel to these natives, they were brutally murdered.

Today many of these same Auca tribesmen are Christians! They are leaders of a small congregation that worships near the spot where the missionaries died. Many educators and government leaders have expressed astonishment at the miraculous transformation of these Indians. How did it happen?

The answer lies in the love expressed to these people by the sister and wife of two of the martyred missionaries. Led by a God of love and not by vengeance, these women labored for years in breaking down the walls of distrust. In time they were able to share the gospel with these tribesmen and to see the love of Christ transform their lives. God's love is the greatest force in the world!

In this powerful thirteenth chapter of Paul's letter to the church at Corinth, the apostle compares this divine love with a number of other highly prized gifts. In every case he demonstrates that no matter what else a person excels in he is of little value unless he possesses the greatest gift of all—God's love. Paul mentions many valuable gifts, but he clearly points out that love is the greatest!

It is both shocking and thrilling to realize that the love that Paul is talking about is neither sentimental nor theoretical. This love is not the cheap billboard or theatrical-style love. It is a deep, quiet, strong love born of God. It is God's love for us and in us!

When God told us to love Him and to love each other, He was stating the most profound principle of life itself. Our mental hospitals are full of men and women who, either intentionally or by accident, are missing this basic ingredient from their lives.

Many of our medical experts today are beginning to realize that love is the answer to many of the physical as well as mental disorders of life.

One of America's leading figures in psychiatry, Dr. Karl Menninger, suggests, "Love is the medicine for our sick old world." At his clinic in Topeka, Kansas, Dr. Menninger instructed his entire staff—doctors, nurses, orderlies, and maintenance workers—that the most important thing they could offer any patient was love. "If people can learn to give and receive love," he said, "they will usually recover from their physical or mental illnesses."

> No cord nor cable can so forcibly draw, or hold so
> fast, as love can do with a twined thread.
>
> BURTON

Dr. Eric Berne, in his best-selling book, *Games People Play,* discusses the tremendous need people have for encouragement, by word and by touch, to "keep their spinal cords from shriveling"—to keep them alive, eager, and confident—and talks about the variety of games people devise to win this sort of healing attention.

> It's love, it's love that makes the world go round.
>
> FRENCH SONG

One man's research disclosed a shocking lack in the handling of infants some years ago. Dr. René A. Spitz was in charge of ninety-one infants in a foundling home. The babies received plenty of good food, clothing, light, air, toys, and competent care, but they lacked one indispensable thing: the attention of a mother. Each nurse cared for ten children, which gave each child the equivalent of one-tenth of a mother. The research showed that this was not enough.

Three months in this home was sufficient to produce marked changes in the babies' personalities. Following up on what became of the motherless foundlings, Dr. Spitz found that thirty percent died in their first year; and twenty-one were so scarred by life they could only be classed as seriously maladjusted. Love is not only important, it is a necessity to our physical, mental, and social well-being.

How pathetic it is, then, that we bypass the gift of love which God holds out to us! How frequently we look up to God and say, "No, thank You!" Our driving self-concern opposes the purposes of almighty God. Little man cuts himself off when he refuses to love; he puts himself out of relationship with God and with others.

> O, there is nothing holier, in this life of ours, than
> the first consciousness of love,—the first fluttering of
> its silken wings.
>
> LONGFELLOW

There is no greater gift available to man than the gift of

love. When we love, God's love is released through us to others.

In the first three verses of 1 Corinthians 13, the apostle Paul presents the deep need for God's love in the Christian's life. He compares and contrasts this great gift with the gifts of speech, prophecy, faith, benevolence, and martyrdom. He demonstrates beyond any shadow of doubt that God's love is the greatest!

LOVE IS GREATER THAN THE ABILITY TO SPEAK WELL

"Though I speak with the tongues of men and of angels, and have not love, I am become as sounding brass, or a tinkling cymbal" (v. 1).

The Corinthians prized the gift of speech. They enjoyed standing in the council and listening to the eloquence of their orators. Demosthenes, Sophocles, Euripides, and other silver-tongued speakers were the idols of the day.

The power of persuasive speech is a great gift, and throughout history powerful eloquence has stirred the masses to heroic deeds and bloody battle. Bernard of Clairvaux spoke, and thousands followed him to the Crusades. Patrick Henry declared his determination to achieve liberty, and a nation arose to fight for freedom. Without question, the spoken word can be a powerful force. But Paul compares words without love to the tuneless crash of a cymbal or the hollow sound of a brass gong without orchestration or melody.

> A vessel is known by the sound, whether it be cracked or not; so men are proved, by their speech, whether they be wise or foolish.
>
> DEMOSTHENES

I have always admired those who are able to speak several languages. Many of us in the English-speaking world are quite limited in our ability to communicate with people of other nations. Because we have little contact with other cultures, we are not forced to learn multiple languages as are many citizens of this world.

But suppose for a moment that you could speak French and German. And suppose you could also converse in Spanish, Russian, and Chinese. Suppose you could speak all the languages of this world. Your ability to communicate would still be worthless if you did not have love.

As the Lord listens to us, what does He hear? Is it the pure symphony of love undefiled, or the blaring of brass and tinkling of cymbals? It would be better that some sermons never be preached and some anthems be left unsung than that love should be missing. Jesus said, "If ye love me, keep my commandments" (John 14:15). He did not tell us to multiply our prayers and praises; He simply commanded us to love one another. "A new commandment I give unto you, that ye love one another; as I have loved you" (John 13:34).

Love is greater than words!

The explosion of Christianity in the Roman Empire was due to the fact that Christians preached the love of Jesus. They preached it by a practical demonstration of love for people. The first believers learned from Jesus Himself. Through His personal association with the despised and downtrodden, and His concern for the poor and afflicted, He showed them how to live a life of love.

The great missionary, David Livingstone, could not always verbally communicate the gospel with the people to whom he ministered, but the people always felt his love. Love has an agility that leaps over language barriers and gets through to people. Love really communicates.

A friend of mine who works with inner-city youth tells the story of a young man from a New York ghetto who spent a week with him at a high school ranch. During the first few days the boy was into all kinds of trouble, but by the end of the camping period he was won by the love of the work crew, counselors, and leaders.

When he returned to the city, he was asked what it was that moved him to accept Christ. He replied, "The way people cared about me. Everybody seemed interested in what was happening to me. Nobody ever loved me like that before."

People will respond to our words when they are woven in love! Although this young man had heard the gospel he had never before seen love in action.

Most men lead lives of quiet desperation

THOREAU

Gina came from one of the thousands of broken homes in the city of Chicago. She started drinking when she was just twelve years of age. She quickly moved on to glue sniffing, and before long she was shooting heroin into her veins.

Sermons were a bore to Gina, but when the people in one of the local churches began paying attention to her as a person, God's love began to reach her. She could not get over the fact that the church people actually wanted her. Only after she had received *their* love was she ready to listen and understand the words that explained God's love for her in Jesus Christ. Gina is just one example of the millions of people who are tired of words without love.

LOVE IS GREATER THAN PROPHECY

"And though I have the gift of prophecy" (v. 2).

Love is not only greater than words, love is greater than prophecy! What a marvelous gift this is! The prophets not only spoke forth God's truth, but in many instances foretold future events. Paul continues to insist, however, that as wonderful as prophecy is, this gift minus love equals nothing.

Throughout the world there is an enormous interest today in trying to look into the future. Nearly fifteen hundred newspapers in this country print horoscope columns every day. Famous seers and so-called prophets have become extremely popular with readers worldwide who are trying to gain some insight into tomorrow. For many, determining the future has become an obsession.

Paul realized the significance of the gift of prophecy. He compares it in this chapter to the greatest possible gifts a man could possess. But he still concludes that the prophetic gift— without love—is meaningless. It cannot compare in significance to the dynamic love of God working in and through the life of a Christian.

D. L. Moody recounted that not until hearing Henry Moorhouse preach on John 3:16 for a solid week did he really understand the greatness of God's love. Richard Ellsworth Day in his biography of Moody entitled *Bush Aglow*, gives Moody's own account of what happened to him at those meetings:

> I never knew up to that time that God loved us so much. This heart of mine began to thaw out; I could not keep back the tears. I just drank it in. . . . I tell you there is one thing that draws above everything else in the world and that is love.

After this happened, Moody, who was already a successful pastor, saw for the first time the secret of a winsome church:

> The churches would soon be filled if outsiders could find that people in them loved them when they came. This love draws sinners! We must win them to us first, then we can win them to Christ. We must get the people to love us, and then turn them over to Christ.

Matthew paints a picture of one calling, "Lord, Lord, have we not prophesied in thy name?" (7:22). The answer is, "I never knew you: depart from me, ye that work iniquity" (v. 23). Love is greater than prophecy and must precede it!

"And understand all mysteries" (v. 2).

Here Paul speaks of divine insight concerning hidden truths. In my travels and my reading, I have met spiritual giants, who challenged me to greater living. Other times I have been keenly disappointed to find people more concerned about hidden mysteries than about needy people. That is a paradox, isn't it? But it's a common one. Too often Christians are concerned about hidden truth, but indifferent about loving difficult people. Skill in unraveling the mysteries of God is very desirable and important, yet this without love for people equals nothing.

It is one thing to know that love is the conquering weapon, the greatest gift. But it is quite another thing to secure it. Moody's account, quoted in *Bush Aglow,* tells how Moorhouse went on to show him that we learn *how to love* from the scriptures.

> I took up that word Love, and I do not know how many weeks I spent in studying the passages in which it occurs, *till at last I could not help loving people.* I had been feeding on Love so long that I was anxious to do everybody good I came in contact with.
>
> I got full of it. It ran out my fingers. You take up the subject of love in the Bible! You will get so full of it that all you have got to do is to open your lips, and a flood of the Love of God flows out.

LOVE IS GREATER THAN KNOWLEDGE

"And all knowledge" (v. 2).

Knowledge is a rare gem, and we never handle this expensive jewel carelessly. Yet there is nothing so hard, dead, and cold as knowledge without love.

> Life is a mission. Every other definition is false and leads all who accept it astray.
>
> MAZZINI

If knowledge were the key that could unlock the door in solving all human problems and suffering, our problems would be over. Mankind today possesses more knowledge than ever before. Scientific learning progresses so rapidly that even the most brilliant cannot keep pace with our achievements.

But the unfortunate truth is that our great strides in knowledge and in understanding the mysteries of the universe have done very little to solve man's problems. In many ways, knowledge by itself compounds our problems rather than solving them.

Knowledge by itself, said the apostle Paul, is still nothing.

Moody was miserable before he felt the power of God's love in his life and in his ministry. His congregations showed signs of falling away. He found himself wondering if the gospel might not need something else to make it attractive to people. While riding on a train from California, where he had attended a Sunday school convention, he recalled young Moorhouse saying to him, four years earlier:

> You are sailing on the wrong track. If you will change your course, and learn to preach God's words instead of your own, He will make you a great power.

Moody had realized then that he had been desperately trying to explain what the Bible teaches before filling his soul with what it says. When Moorhouse had left Chicago, Moody had not followed the new light; he had taken a course of reading. And when he selected a text and started to preach, he immediately departed from it. Now, sitting on the train, he recalled with new meaning what an old gentleman in Boston had told him years before: "Young man, when you speak again, honor the Holy Ghost."

That summer Moody made the rewarding committal of giving even his ignorance to Christ, and new life flooded his church. Even the heat of August did not keep the people away. Moody realized humbly that power was present now—power that had never been there in the parade of his own knowledge.

Love ignores high-sounding explanations and goes to work. Love gets us in gear with God and the times. Love transforms our doctrine into power. Love adds feet to facts, resulting in action. The need of this hour, as much as Moody's, is for the marriage of love to knowledge.

Moody's sound advice to his successor was this: "Dr. Erdman, give the people the importance of love. If they are right here, they will be right 95 percent of the time."

A churchwoman once confessed to me, "I have been a Christian for twenty years now. During that time I have read many books on winning others, yet I do not know of anyone that I have led to the Lord. I have memorized Scripture and know how to meet the objections of the unconverted, but still I have brought no one to a decision. Why have I been so useless?"

My answer surprised her. "You are a fruitless Christian," I told her, "because your eyes are dry."

"I don't understand," she said, and so I added, "You have failed not for want of knowledge but for lack of love for people. When you really love someone, you will care enough to weep for them."

God's Word promises that, "He that goeth forth and weepeth, bearing precious seed, shall doubtless come again with rejoicing, bringing his sheaves with him" (Psalm 126:6).

This lady returned home to read the Scriptures and to pray. As she prayed, her heart became strangely warmed. Her unbelieving sister came vividly to her mind, she got up from her knees to find her, and with genuine tears threw her arms around her sister and admitted in love, "More than anything in this world, I want you to be a Christian!" They came together to the meeting that night, and when I gave an invitation, the two of them walked up together to respond to the appeal.

Sometimes we are so tactful that we fail to make contact. Are we more concerned about what people think than about what God thinks? Paul went even farther when he wrote, "I could wish that myself were accursed from Christ for my brethren, my kinsmen according to the flesh" (Romans 9:3). That is shocking! What is Paul saying? He is expressing his willingness to be forever damned if that would save others. What a staggering illustration of love! This is a redemptive love very few of us know much about. Knowledge is extremely important, especially in our age, yet it must be born in love to be eternal.

In 1 Corinthians 8:1 Paul reminds us, "Knowledge puffeth up, but love edifieth." At times we witness a dichotomy between knowledge and love. This need not be! I have witnessed students who, although they have accumulated a great deal of knowledge, have a scarcity of love.

We need to strive for knowledge that is on fire. Our goal must be academic excellence that is immersed in the love of Jesus Christ.

Knowledge without love is dead! Knowledge with love is dynamic and irresistible!

One day some years ago I went to visit a man who was called the toughest man in town. As I attempted to share my knowledge of God with him, he cursed the church, the Bible, and me. Then he threatened to throw me out bodily if I ever returned to his home again. As I made my watchful retreat, I said quietly, "Mr. Baldwin, God loves you, and I love you."

I was not prepared for what happened. Almost instantly he melted. He slipped to his knees and wept uncontrollably as he emptied out a heart full of hatred and sin. It was God's love that did it. That rough railroader was gloriously changed by the gospel. Knowledge without love is impotent, but together they generate tremendous force.

LOVE IS GREATER THAN FAITH

"And though I have all faith, so that I could remove mountains, and have not love, I am nothing" (v. 2).

The faith referred to here is that of getting things done. Faith is a great gift. In fact, without faith we cannot please God.

When Jesus' disciples were not able to cast a demon out of a man who had been brought to them, they questioned the Lord saying, "Why could not we cast him out?" Jesus answered them and said, "Because of your unbelief; for verily I say unto you, If ye have faith as a grain of mustard seed, ye shall say unto this mountain, Move from here to yonder place; and it shall move; and nothing shall be impossible unto you" (Matthew 17:19-20).

Make no mistake, faith is important! It is the foundation upon which love can build. Faith is first, even though love is last. An individual must come to Christ in faith before he can know anything of God's love.

But—faith *without* love is nothing.

An exciting breakthrough came to a group of New England pastors who met in Boston for three days in a study of love that ignited their faith. One of the men who attended said, "We listened, learned, and loved. We were reconciled and brought together! The world will never really believe in the power of Christ until it can see us one in love and appreciation, respecting each other as men, attempting to discover ever more clearly the power of the risen Christ."

Without the love of Christ nourishing our behavior, we bring the powerlessness of a dead faith to a dying world. Paul wrote to the Ephesians, "That Christ may dwell in your hearts by faith; that ye, being rooted and grounded in love, May be able to comprehend, with all saints, what is the breadth, and length, and depth, and height, And to know the love of Christ, which passeth knowledge, that ye might be filled with all the fullness of God" (3:17-19).

Paul was so emphatically the apostle of faith that his conclusion is all the more convincing. Faith is great, but love is greater. Faith has priority, but love has preeminence. Faith is first, but love is last. Faith connects the soul with God, and God is love. Faith is the means that God uses to bring us into His love, but faith without love places us in life's minus column!

LOVE IS GREATER THAN BENEVOLENCE

"And though I bestow all my goods to feed the poor, and though I give my body to be burned, and have not love, it profiteth me nothing" (v. 3).

All of us have given to help the poor: a dinner to the hungry, a donation to the underprivileged, a dollar to the cripple as he stretches out his tin cup. Prosperity imposes obligation. To have should mean to help. The needy are all about us, but often benevolence is an act of relief for a guilty conscience. It is too easy in our prosperous times to write a check or dismiss our responsibility for caring. Even the emperors of Rome gave lavishly on special holidays to keep the masses under their control. They gave bread for their stomachs, they provided the circus for their entertainment. But they gave without loving. How humiliating would be a revelation of the motives for our own deeds!

Too often we give to others, not out of a sense of gratitude to God for what He has given to us, but because of a feeling of obligation. With a level of personal wealth that is higher than ever before, psychologists are finding that many people harbor a guilt complex that stems from their accumulation of material possessions. These people will give because they feel guilty over all they possess.

For others, philanthropy or the giving of gifts is a means of personal recognition. A man may make a donation to a cause because he desires another's praise. Like the self-righteous man in Jesus' parable, he gives so that all can see.

The pattern of life in the early church indicates a method of giving much different from these. Those first Christians had learned from Christ that it was impossible to belong to each other and yet be indifferent to the needs of a member. The phrase used in Acts, "in common," seems to indicate their belief that God's gifts were meant to supply the needs of all, and should be shared with others.

What was not essential for their own needs was shared with the poor. As Bernard F. Meyer says, "We cannot but think that Jesus often invited the poor to eat with Him, rather than giving them a backdoor handout."

> I expect to pass through this world but once. Any good therefore that I can do, or any kindness that I can show to any fellow creature, let me do it now. Let me not defer or neglect it, for I shall not pass this way again.
>
> ANONYMOUS

This quality of giving can only spring from love. It is neither an action pasted on to satisfy a requirement, nor an excuse to buy our way from personal involvement. The love which is already present within us, because God is there, bears fruit in our sharing our resources gladly. On the other hand, the Pharisees sounded the trumpets so everyone would notice that they were giving. The Bible says, "They have their reward" (Matthew 6:2). It is not so much what we give, but how we give it. We can give without loving, but we cannot love without giving. Love is greater than any act of benevolence.

LOVE IS GREATER THAN MARTYRDOM

"And though I give my body to be burned, and have not love, it profiteth me nothing" (v. 3).

Martyrdom is farther from our experience today than it was at the time Paul was writing to the Corinthians. Undoubtedly there were Christians in Corinth who suffered the fiery faggots and the lion's teeth. In those days, hundreds endured physical violence because of their deep love for Christ. This text suggests, however, that martyrdom could result from something other than consecration. Perhaps it could be fanatical devotion to a cause rather than love for Christ. Martyrdom may be more out of principle than out of love.

The war in Vietnam produced some spectacular instances of

martyrdom, such as the young man who set fire to himself in Washington and burned to death in protest as people watched helplessly. The Buddhist monks who became fiery pillars to a pacifistic principle were modern-day martyrs for a cause.

Charles L. Allen, in his book, *The Miracle of Love,* suggests that perhaps Paul had yet another thought in mind when he spoke of giving his body to be burned. "This was a day when slavery was commonly practiced. Just as ranchers brand cattle today, human beings were branded as slaves in that day. The hot iron was applied to their flesh and those men wore the stigma the balance of their lives. 'Though I give my body to become a branded slave . . .' This is sacrifice in its most complete form. Yet—even such sacrifice is profitless without love."

A generation ago there was a common plea for young people to love Christ enough to die for Him. Today the plea more commonly assumes that it takes as much or more courage to live for Him. To live a life in relationship to those around us is no easy calling. It calls for every ounce of commitment we can uncover. Living the love of God is the greatest challenge, the highest calling to which a human being can respond. Someone has said, "Love is appealing, but its practice is appallingly difficult."

We humans are crafty creatures who rationalize so much that it is difficult to decide what our real motives are. Will you try an experiment? Stop reading for a moment. Look over your life. Analyze your failures, your restless spirit, your dissatisfaction. You will probably discover that love is the missing link. Certainly a portion of the good news of the gospel lies in the difference Christ promised us as we come to Him. We need to heed the advice of Scripture, "Seek ye first the kingdom of God, and his righteousness; and all these things shall be added unto you" (Matthew 6:33)

John Calvin, commenting on these verses, said, "For where love is wanting, the beauty of all virtue is mere tinsel, is empty sound, is not worth a straw, nay more, is offensive and disgusting."

Let me summarize this entire chapter with a simple yet potent equation: *Life minus love equals zero!*

SUGGESTED PRAYER

Thy love is greater than all the gifts of the Spirit. Take my lips and talk through them; take my mind and think through it; take my knowledge and set it on fire; take my heart and flood it with thy love. Love this world through me. Amen.

REMINDERS

• Paul mentions many valuable gifts, but he clearly points out that love is the greatest!

• We can give without loving, but we cannot love without giving.

• "A vessel is known by the sound whether it be cracked or not; so men are proved, by their speech, whether they be wise or foolish." DEMOSTHENES

• "Most men lead lives of quiet desperation." THOREAU

• *Life minus love equals zero!*

1 CORINTHIANS 13

Christian love—the highest and best gift

If I speak with the eloquence of men and of angels, but have no love, I become no more than blaring brass or crashing cymbal If I have the gift of foretelling the future and hold in my mind not only all human knowledge but the very secrets of God, and if I also have that absolute faith which can move mountains, but have no love, I amount to nothing at all. If I dispose of all that I possess, yes, even if I give my own body to be burned, but have no love, I achieve precisely nothing.

This love of which I speak is slow to lose patience—it looks for a way of being constructive. It is not possessive: it is neither anxious to impress nor does it cherish inflated ideas of its own importance.

Love has good manners and does not pursue selfish advantage. It is not touchy. It does not keep account of evil or gloat over the wickedness of other people. On the contrary, it shares the joy of those who live by the truth.

Love knows no limit to its endurance, no end to its trust, no fading of its hope; it can outlast anything. Love never fails.

All gifts except love will be superseded one day

For if there are prophecies they will be fulfilled and done with, if there are "tongues" the need for them will disappear, if there is knowledge it will be swallowed up in truth. For our knowledge is always incomplete and our prophecy is always incomplete, and when the complete comes, that is the end of the incomplete.

When I was a little child I talked and felt and thought like a little child. Now that I am a man I have finished with childish things.

At present we are men looking at puzzling reflections in a mirror. The time will come when we shall see reality whole and face to face! At present all I know is a little fraction of the truth, but the time will come when I shall know it as fully as God has known me!

In this life we have three lasting qualities—faith, hope and love. But the greatest of them is love.

The New Testament in Modern English by J. B. Phillips, rev. ed. (New York: Macmillan, 1972). Copyright J. B. Phillips 1958, 1960, 1972. All rights reserved. Used by permission of the publisher.

4

WHAT IS LOVE LIKE?

"Love suffereth long, and is kind; love envieth not; love vaunteth not itself, is not puffed up" (v. 4).

Do you know the meaning of love?

Throughout the centuries hundreds of books have been written and thousands of songs have been sung in an attempt to define the magical four-letter word—love.

Some people say that love defies description. And yet, as the artist blends colors to produce a beautiful painting, so Paul in this chapter combines the many characteristics of love as seen in Jesus Christ to give us a beautiful picture of love.

From Bethlehem's manger to the mount of ascension, the life of Christ was a life of unselfish love. Every characteristic of love given in this chapter is seen in the person of Christ, and the achievement of these same characteristics should be the goal of every Christian.

"Love suffereth long and is kind" (v. 4).

People are always hungry for kindness. Kindness might be defined as the expression of a friendly sympathetic nature. Wordsworth described it as, "the best portion of a good man's life." The word *kindness* comes from kindred or kin, and implies affection to those who are our flesh and blood.

Paul suggests that kindness is one of the distinguishing characteristics of true Christian love. It is also a picture of God's love toward us. In spite of our indifferences and unloveliness,

51

He keeps on loving us. At times we may, as this verse suggests, suffer long, but the question is, Are we kind?

> Kindness is the golden chain by which society is bound together
>
> GOETHE

A pastor friend in Pennsylvania discovered two women living near his church who were lonely and in need of help. Because he had heard of their odd behavior, he asked one of the ladies in his congregation to visit these women. The woman possessed a lot of courage and kindness, but still felt apprehensive as she walked up the path to the run-down house. When she knocked on the door, one of the women opened the door and asked why she had come. Assuring the woman that she wanted only to be of help, she was asked to come in and was led to a bedroom where the woman's mother lay, frowning and suspicious. As the mother began to question her, the visitor remembered all the neighborhood stories she had heard about these women. She became frightened and wondered why she had ever agreed to make the visit.

But as they talked, she began thinking about the love that Christ expressed to women just like these two. "God loves these women," she thought, "and I love them too!" What a change she felt come over her as she began to really listen and show concern! Before leaving the house she even put her arms around the big, straggly-haired woman and gave her a hug and a kiss. Tears came to the old woman's eyes, and her frown was changed to a beautiful smile. Here was the kindness of Christ reaching out to someone starved for love; and it opened the way for kindness to be multiplied by many others in the church.

Two families donated coal to heat the house; another gave a refrigerator; some contributed clothes; the elderly mother was given badly needed hospital care. Children sent cards and baked cookies. One man began to take care of the women's lawn. A neighbor offered the use of her telephone whenever needed. Another woman took time to drive the daughter to the market for groceries.

Eventually the new friendships included a time of praying and Bible study. And before long the two women received Jesus Christ as their personal Lord and Saviour, all because they had been shown the love of Jesus Christ.

When the visits to this home first began, the women often asked, "Why do you care? Why do you come?" What an evidence of the indwelling presence of Jesus Christ we can present when we express to others the warm loving kindness that is characteristic of our Saviour.

Divine love is kind even when misunderstood. Love knows how to take sorrow and heartache victoriously. The Greek verb meaning "is kind" implies active service. Our old flesh is hasty, hotheaded, and unkind; but God's love is very different.

I remember a situation some years ago when I was misunderstood and criticized by people who I expected would know better. I desperately wanted to retaliate, or at least to present my version of the story. By bulldog determination, I clenched my fist, bit my lip, and managed to keep my mouth closed. But I was not gracious, and I did not display much kindness.

A large part of being kind is the patient willingness to put up with the abuse or ridicule that comes our way. Usually that patience is needed most just when it is exhausted. So often our tolerance level wears thin at the wrong time, and our spirit of kindness melts away. Real love is kind, it is patient, and it never gives up.

> There is no such thing as being a gentleman at important moments; it is at unimportant moments that a man is a gentleman. . . . If once his mind is possessed in any strong degree with the knowledge that he is a gentleman he will soon cease to be one.
>
> CHESTERTON

Jesus Christ spent His life ministering to others. For thirty-three years He went about doing kind deeds, ministering to the sick, feeding the hungry, comforting the bereaved, always helping others! And although He was often misunderstood, misused, and rejected, Jesus was kind.

The Saviour was longsuffering with His weak-willed disciples who disappointed Him so often. He was merciful to the despised and the mentally disturbed. He was longsuffering with Pilate, with the Roman centurion, with the crucified thief. Jesus suffered long and was kind even in His dying hours. After the nails had done their ugly work, He cried out, saying, "Father, forgive them; for they know not what they do" (Luke 23:34).

This kind of love that Paul describes goes beyond human understanding, yet this is the kind of love God would manifest through us. When Stephen, one of the early church deacons, was being stoned to death, he prayed, "Lord, lay not this sin to their charge" (Acts 7:60). What kind of love is this? It is a constancy of love amid neglect, ignorance, lack of appreciation, and even undeserved violence. This kind of love is possible only through Jesus Christ. He gives us the capacity to live and to love.

Someone has changed the words of the hymn, "Are Ye Able," to read this way:

> Able to suffer without complaining;
> To be misunderstood without explaining;
>
> Able to give without receiving,
> To be ignored without grieving;
>
> Able to ask without commanding,
> To love despite misunderstanding;
>
> Able to turn to the Lord for guarding;
> Able to wait for His own rewarding.

A love that suffers long and is kind, is power beyond our natural capacity. It is only as we experience God's love flowing through us that we can know the true meaning of love that suffers long and is kind.

How much genuine concern do you have for other people? How willing are you to put the desires of another above your own? How hard would you work to spare a friend disappointment or sorrow? Are you willing to go an extra mile, or to turn the other cheek? Do you go out of your way to be cooperative, to try to get along with others?

The story is told of two mountain goats who approached one another on a narrow ledge. Realizing that there was no room to pass, they reared and bucked, but neither budged. They backed up, charged, and locked horns again, but each held his ground. Again they parted and charged; then like the Rock of Gibraltar they stood unmoveable. Finally the sensible one knelt down, and let the other one climb over him. Then they both went merrily on their way. Sometimes we too must let people walk over us. Love is magnanimous.

Dr. Harry Ironside used to tell of a young man who disrupted a church business meeting by shouting, "I want my rights, I want my rights." An elderly member of the church who was hard of hearing responded, "Did I hear our young friend say he wanted his rights? If he received his rights he would be judged and sent to perdition. Jesus Christ went to the cross to die for his 'wrongs' and make him right."

With that the younger man apologized for acting in the energy of the flesh, and the meeting continued. Christian love is and must always be magnanimous!

"Love envieth not" (v. 4).

"Envy," says the Latin proverb, "is the enemy of honor." Envy has been defined as the sorrow of fools. Solomon described it as "the rottenness of the bones" (Proverbs 14:30). William Shakespeare spoke of envy specifically as "the green sickness."

Paul declares that true Christian love is never envious or jealous of anyone or anything. It is not possessive.

Envy and jealousy are deadly in the life of a Christian. It was jealousy that caused Joseph to be sold into Egypt. His half-brothers were discontented because he was the favored son of Jacob. Cain's envy led him to commit murder. Envy was also demonstrated by the elder brother in the story of the prodigal son. When he heard the rejoicing over his wayward brother, the Scripture says, "He was angry, and would not go in" (Luke 15:28). Both brothers missed the father's love—one because he was rebellious, and the other because he was envious. Envy is essentially satanic whenever and wherever it appears.

Envy exists in almost everyone. It is a disease that disturbs the mind and consumes the body. Some people can even become physically ill because of envy.

"Wrath is cruel, and anger is outrageous," wrote Solomon, "but who is able to stand before envy?" (Proverbs 27:4). Envy is relentless in its pursuit of the human heart. Envy observes no holidays; it works continually. Envy is discontentment at the good fortunes of others. Envy says, "If I cannot eat, then I want all others to starve. If I cannot see in one eye, I want you to be blind in both eyes." Envy is hatred without a cure. It blurs our vision and prevents us from living life victoriously.

According to James, jealousy is a characteristic of earthly wisdom which results in confusion and disorder and all kinds of evil: "But if ye have bitter envying and strife in your hearts, glory not, and lie not against the truth. This wisdom descendeth not from above, but is earthly, sensual, demoniacal. For where envying and strife are, there is confusion and every evil work" (James 3:14-16).

King Saul envied David to such a degree that he lost all control of himself and tried to kill David. Envy is usually a trait of the carnal or unregenerate soul. In contrast, love rejoices when others excel. Jonathan, Saul's son, could have been af-

flicted with the same satanic disease as his father; but he de-
throned envy wth love. "He loved him [David] as he loved his
own soul" (1 Samuel 20:17).

The only way to cure envy is to pray sincerely for the one
of whom you are envious. Paul plainly tells us, "For all the law
is fulfilled in one word, even in this; Thou shalt love thy neighbor as thyself. But if ye bite and devour one another, take heed
that ye be not consumed one of another" (Galatians 5:14-15).
I am sure that there are some people we *must* pray for, or else
our envy will consume us.

The Christians in the church of Corinth were reprimanded
by Paul because of this very problem. They were saved, but
Christ was not supreme in their lives. "For ye are yet carnal:
for whereas there is among you envying, and strife, and divi-
sions, are ye not carnal, and walk as men?" (1 Corinthians
3:3). They had not yet learned to control this deadly weapon—
envy—and they were living immature and defeated Christian
lives.

"Love vaunteth not itself, is not puffed up" (v. 4).

Falling in love is an exciting experience. We all know that
strong sweep of emotion which leads us to forget ourselves and
to promise our beloved anything. We meet someone who helps
us leap over the walls of our own self-centeredness. We stop
being concerned about ourselves and start thinking only of our
loved one. Without expecting it or working toward it, we spontaneously and magnificently fulfill the law of God (toward one
person) by loving someone else as much as we do ourselves!

This is a spectacular happening! There is no desire or temp-
tation to "puff" ourselves. Our only concern is to build up the
beloved. Our pride in her company, her attention, her abilities,
is radiant, and everyone recognizes it in our behavior.

The hitch arises when we discover after a week or a month
or a year that this high and lofty condition is temporary, or at
best intermittent. The old self, which we thought we had set

aside in our love for another, rears up and starts begging for attention, for flattery, for recognition. Only as our human love bows before the love of God and invites His humility and His grace into that relationship, can it become a dependable and lasting love.

In one of Aesop's fables, a fly sat upon the axle of a chariot wheel and said, "What a dust do I raise!" Empty trucks always make the most noise. The proud have an exaggerated idea of their own importance. Their primary interest is in themselves.

> The ears of barley that bear the richest grain always
> hang the lowest.
>
> ANONYMOUS

"Nothing sets a person so much out of the devil's reach as humility," said the great preacher Jonathan Edwards. Pride is one of the Christian's greatest enemies. It is often at the bottom of our biggest blunders. A young Scottish minister once stepped into the pulpit with pride and complete self-confidence, but the sermon he delivered affected his congregation like a double dose of sleeping pills. The message was a failure, and he knew it. As he left the pulpit in defeat, an old lady whispered, "Son, if you had gone up the way you came down, you would have come down the way you went up!" Love is humble. It does not boast about itself.

> They that know God will be humble and they that
> know themselves cannot be proud.
>
> JOHN FLAVEL

A proud and puffed-up spirit only indicates that a person does not have a proper self-image. When we see ourselves as God sees us, we cannot help but be humbled.

When a committee from Jerusalem asked John the Baptist if he were the Messiah, he answered them simply, "I am not." "Then, who are you?" they asked. John said, "I am a voice" (John 1:19-23). He plainly told them that he was not the way, but just the messenger to show the way. John was so filled with love for Jesus that self-conscious pride was impossible. "He must increase" said John, "but I must decrease" (John 3:30).

Divine love does not parade for the applause of the crowd, but places itself below all others. God keeps His best gifts on the lower shelves. Humility precedes honor as "an haughty spirit before a fall" (Proverbs 16:18). The apostle Paul said, "knowledge puffeth up, but love edifieth" (1 Corinthians 8:1). The word "puff" is defined as any sudden or short blast of wind. The love of Christ is not sudden or brief; it is eternal. Love builds forever.

A missionary once was translating the word "pride" into a native language. To properly convey the meaning she wrote, "the ears are too far apart." Pride was simply an inflated head.

Love is not big-headed; it is big-hearted. The greater a person's ability, the less boasting he needs to do; and conversely, the less ability one has, the more noise he has to make about it. Remember, empty trucks always make the most noise. Divine love need not be inflated, for it allows us to see ourselves as we really are in the sight of God.

SUGGESTED PRAYER

Lord, make me an instrument of Thy peace. Where there is hatred, let there be love; where there is injury, pardon; where there is doubt, faith; where there is despair, hope; where there is darkness, light; where there is sadness, joy. O Divine Master, grant that I may not seek so much to be consoled as to console; to be understood as to understand; to be loved as to love. For it is in giving that we receive, it is in pardon that we are pardoned, it is in dying that we are born to Eternal Life.

FRANCIS OF ASSISI

REMINDERS

- "Love suffereth long, and is kind; love envieth not; love vaunteth not itself, is not puffed up" (v. 4).

- Every characteristic of love given in this chapter is seen in the person of Christ, and the achievement of these same characteristics should be the goal of every Christian.

- The only way to cure envy is to pray sincerely for the one of whom you are envious.

- Divine love does not parade for the applause of the crowd, but places itself below all others.

- God keeps His best gifts on the lower shelves.

- Love is not big-headed; it is big-hearted.

- Empty trucks always make the most noise.

1 CORINTHIANS 13

If I had the gift of being able to speak in other languages without learning them, and could speak in every language there is in all of heaven and earth, but didn't love others, I would only be making noise. ² If I had the gift of prophecy and knew all about what is going to happen in the future, knew everything about everything, but didn't love others, what good would it do? Even if I had the gift of faith so that I could speak to a mountain and make it move, I would still be worth nothing at all without love. ³ If I gave everything I have to poor people, and if I were burned alive for preaching the Gospel but didn't love others, it would be of no value whatever.

⁴ Love is very patient and kind, never jealous or envious, never boastful or proud, ⁵ never haughty or selfish or rude. Love does not demand its own way. It is not irritable or touchy. It does not hold grudges and will hardly even notice when others do it wrong. ⁶ It is never glad about injustice, but rejoices whenever truth wins out. ⁷ If you love someone you will be loyal to him no matter what the cost. You will always believe in him, always expect the best of him, and always stand your ground in defending him.

⁸ All the special gifts and powers from God will someday come to an end, but love goes on forever. Someday prophecy, and speaking in unknown languages, and special knowledge—these gifts will disappear. ⁹ Now we know so little, even with our special gifts, and the preaching of those most gifted is still so poor. ¹⁰ But when we have been made perfect and complete, then the need for these inadequate special gifts will come to an end, and they will disappear.

¹¹ It's like this: when I was a child I spoke and thought and reasoned as a child does. But when I became a man my thoughts grew far beyond those of my childhood, and now I have put away the childish things. ¹² In the same way, we can see and understand only a little about God now, as if we were peering at His reflection in a poor mirror; but someday we are going to see Him in His completeness, face to face. Now all that I know is hazy and blurred, but then I will see everything clearly, just as clearly as God sees into my heart right now.

¹³ There are three things that remain—faith, hope, and love— and the greatest of these is love.

The Living Bible Paraphrased (Wheaton, Ill.: Tyndale, 1971). Used by permission.

5

LOVE AND THE WAY YOU ACT

"Doth not behave itself unseemly, seeketh not her own, is not easily provoked, thinketh no evil" (v. 5).

In our sophisticated society we tend to think of our conduct as a highly polished way of life. We observe the important rules of etiquette, congratulate our friends on their accomplishments and generally put on quite a show of concern for our neighbors. We may even smile at people we dislike or exchange greetings with our enemies. We invite the new neighbors in for coffee or give Thanksgiving baskets to the poor, and then we pat ourselves on the back for being so loving and kind.

But the love that the apostle Paul talks about in 1 Corinthians 13 is a much more difficult way of life. True love "doth not behave itself unseemly" (v. 5). According to Paul, true divine love is never selfish. It never behaves in a rude manner.

COURTESY IS LOVE IN ACTION

"Doth not behave itself unseemly" (v. 5).

We know it is polite for a man to stand when a woman enters the room; to say thank you for a gift. We know that a gentleman removes his hat upon entering a house, and that well-behaved children hop up to offer their seats to adults coming into the room. But many of these things we do merely out of a feeling of social responsibility. Sometimes they become a chore or duty to us, and we find little joy in doing them.

63

The test of good manners is to be able to put up
pleasantly with bad ones.

WENDELL WILKIE

What a difference it makes when we truly love someone!
How we jump to do little things that are signals of our loving
attention! When we love someone, we put that person upper-
most in our thoughts and actions. Someone has defined polite-
ness as "love in trifles." To do little things for others, in a way
that is genuine, is to prove one's love. Love does not behave
in a discourteous manner. Greed does; selfishness does; fear
does—but not love.

Analyze yourself the next time you are delayed in a traffic
jam and lean on the horn. Think of what's wrong inside of you
when you try to crowd in front of another grocery shopper at
the check-out stand. What is pushing you? Courtesy does not
push other people around; love expresses itself by making the
way easier for someone. Love kneels to serve others.

> Of Courtesy, it is much less
> Than Courage of Heart or Holiness,
> Yet in my walks it seems to me
> That the Grace of God is in Courtesy.

HILAIRE BELLAS

I once knew a husband who had entered into a new relationship with Christ and wanted to share it with his wife. Years
before, he had decided that one chore he would not do around
the house was carry out the garbage—he would do anything
else gladly, but not that.

Now, as he began asking the Lord how he could get through
to his wife, there seemed to be no approach that was not pre-
faced by that garbage sack sitting by the back door. So finally
he stooped down, picked the bag up, and carried it out to the
alley. His love for both God and his wife had grown past the
point where he had to prove his superiority. He was free to
become a garbage carrier in love.

Life is short, but there is always time for courtesy.

EMERSON

The one who allows the love of Christ to control him is not hard or harsh, crude or rude, rough or tough. He is gentle and courteous. While the word courteous originally came from "court" and suggested the manners which prevailed in the palaces of kings and queens, eventually it came to mean consideration for others.

Paul suggests this rule: "Let each esteem others better than themselves" (Philippians 2:3). A. T. Williams translates it, "Stop acting from motives of selfish strife of petty ambition, but in humility practice treating one another as your superiors."

No man is an island, entire of itself, every man is a piece of the continent.

JOHN DONNE

One of the proofs of our love is the helping hand we hold out to a needy world—beginning under our very own roof.

Courtesy springs from love as the flowers spring from the fertile soil in the woods. Regardless of background, a Christian man will become a gentleman and a Christian woman, a lady. Why? Because when God's love is planted in us, we grow to be like Christ. Love transforms the commonest of mortals.

We live in a world where everyone likes to toot his own horn. We seem to learn from the time we grab the blocks away from a playmate, that we can shove a little bit here and pull a little bit there and somehow come out on top. One-upmanship is the game of the day. "Get ahead," the world says. "Step on anybody you like as you climb to the top." Whether we are heading for the presidency of the PTA, or the manager's spot in our department, subconscious schemes almost always form in our brains as we figure out how we can make ourselves look better than the man or woman next to us. We tell ourselves that if we do not push ourselves forward and use others to further our own goals, we may be scoffed at as shiftless victims of inferiority complexes who just cannot make the grade.

> Whenever you are too selfishly looking out for your own interest, you have only one person working for you—yourself. When you help a dozen other people with their problems, you have a dozen people working with you.
>
> WILLIAM B. GIVEN, JR.

How completely different from God's approach! Paul described Jesus as One who was willing to make Himself of no reputation, one who humbled Himself as He became obedient unto death (Philippians 2:7-8). Jesus Christ is the supreme example of selfless love.

Manhattan Project Number Two is the story of a man who had to learn to be a servant for Christ's sake. Red Cap 42 carried people's bags for forty years. He was so disgusted with his role in life that whenever anyone asked him his occupation, he would say he was "in the leather business." He hated everybody because having to carry others' baggage made him feel he was not as good as they were.

After Christ came into his life, Red Cap 42's whole outlook changed. He stayed in the same business, but he was carrying bags for God now, and he began talking with God all the time about his customers. Person after person sensed this elderly man's attitude. Many came into a personal relationship with the Saviour through the witness of red cap, Ralston Young. They began to meet together with him for prayer in an empty railroad coach parked on a siding.

Before long a group of businessmen rented an office for Ralston Young on New York's Madison Avenue, where they could have their regular prayer meetings. They formed a board, and since the atomic bomb had been Manhattan Project Number One, they named their prayer project, Manhattan Project Number Two. God had used Ralston Young greatly in his position as a bag carrier.

"Seeketh not its own" (v. 5).

Love does not push itself into the limelight. Love does not strive for place or position. In God's program, we stoop to conquer; we kneel to rise. The way up is the way down. The secret is the surrendering of our will to the will of God, so that His way becomes our way.

> Do you want to enter what people call "the higher life"? Then go a step lower down.
>
> ANDREW MURRAY

Joseph of the Old Testament went down into the pit, down into the slavery, down into the dungeon for thirteen years; then, because he had done his work well and faithfully, he was lifted up and eventually became the ruler of all Egypt.

We must go down before we go up; we must go deeper before we go farther. Love walks softly and seeks not her own way. The greatest happiness in life comes from giving, not from getting. "Bear ye one another's burdens, and so fulfill the law of Christ" (Galatians 6:2).

> The greatest difficulty with the world is not its ability to produce, but its unwillingness to share.
>
> ROY L. SMITH

The Bible indicates that one of the signs of the end times is selfishness. "This know also, that in the last days perilous times shall come. For men shall be lovers of their own selves, covetous, boasters, proud, blasphemers, disobedient to parents, unthankful, unholy" (2 Timothy 3:1-2).

One of the chief characteristics of an egotist is self-centeredness. The ego-driven man or woman thinks of himself as supreme and all others as nothing. But if God's love is in us, we do not act that way. God's love is different. It is not a circle, but more like outstretched arms that reach people wherever they are and lifts them up.

> Master selfishness or it will master you.

> He who lives to benefit himself confers on the world
> a benefit when he dies.
>
> TERTULLIAN

"Is not easily provoked" (v. 5).

Irritability is one of the products of our nervous atomic space age. We rush here and there; we don't know where we're going, but we're already ten minutes late. I am amused when I watch shoppers in a department store get excited because they missed one section of a revolving door. The center of irritability is self. The test of your spirituality is not measured at the Sunday worship service, but at home when your son kicks his pajamas under the bed instead of placing them in the hamper, or when the coats are hung on the floor instead of in the closet. The validity of faith is not discovered at the Lord's table on Sunday, but at the breakfast table on Monday. We entertain the stranger with smiles, while our loved ones are hurt by neglect and familiarity. The toughest place to demonstrate love is at home.

> Irritation in the heart of a believer is always an invi-
> tation to the devil to stand by.
>
> ANONYMOUS

Paul writes that love is not provoked. The word "easily" is often seized as an excuse for letting off steam, but this word is not found in any of original manuscripts. Probably some of the translators in 1611 thought Paul was going a bit too far, so they added the word "easily" to the King James Version!

I know of a little boy who went riding with his daddy. The father drove with little regard for anyone. He fussed and fumed, bellowed and shouted at the other drivers as he drove through town. Finally they arrived home. Later that same day, the boy was out in the car with his mother. As they drove peacefully along, the boy said, "Mom, where are all the idiots?"

"Idiots?" exclaimed the mother.

"Yes, this morning when I was out with daddy, we met seven of them!"

Love is the best ointment for irritability, right where we live. This sin has spoiled the peace of many homes. Some people are harder to get along with than a bale of barbed wire.

There is a tradition that Jonathan Edwards, third president of Princeton and one of America's great preachers, had a daughter with an uncontrollable temper. But, as is often the case, this fault was not known to many people outside of her family.

One day a young man fell in love with this daughter and asked to marry her.

"You can't have her," was the abrupt answer of Jonathan Edwards.

"But I love her," the young man replied.

"You can't have her," repeated Edwards.

"But she loves me," replied the young man.

Again Edwards said, "You can't have her."

"Why?" asked the young man.

"Because she is not worthy of you."

"But," he asked, "she is a Christian, isn't she?"

"Yes, she is a Christian, but the grace of God can live with some people with whom no one else could ever live!"

The secret of the temper is more than self-control; it is Christ-control. All of us have dynamite in the cellar, and whenever we walk without God and the power of His love, we must expect explosions.

A woman said to her pastor, "I lose my temper, but it's all over in a minute." The pastor answered, "And so is the atom bomb. But think of the damage it produces!" When you lose control of yourself in any way, you really lose the ability to think and act as a rational human being. You become in a sense subhuman.

A bad temper is something you never lose by loosing.

"A wholesome tongue is a tree of life: but perverseness therein is a breach in the spirit" (Proverbs 15:4). Paul instructed

Timothy, "The servant of the Lord must not strive, but be
gentle unto all men, apt to teach, patient, In meekness instruct-
ing those that oppose him" (2 Timothy 2:24-25).

Henry Drummond spoke about temper in his address, "The
Greatest Thing in the World:"

> It is the intermittent fever which bespeaks unintermittent
> disease within; the occasional bubble escaping to the sur-
> face which betrays some rottenness underneath; a sample
> of the most hidden products of the soul dropped involun-
> tarily when off one's guard; in a word, the lightning form
> of a hundred hideous and unchristian sins. A want of
> patience, a want of kindness, a want of generosity, a want
> of courtesy, a want of unselfishness, are all instantaneously
> symbolized in one flash of temper.
>
> Hence it is not enough to deal with the temper. We must
> go to the source and change the inmost nature. . . . Souls
> are made sweet not by taking the acid fluids out but by
> putting something in—a great love, a new spirit, the Spirit
> of Christ. . . . This only can eradicate what is wrong, work
> a chemical change, renovate . . . the inner man.

"Thinketh no evil" (v. 5).

Love is optimistic; it looks at people in the best light. Love
thinks constructively as it senses the grand possibilities in other
people. What a delightful condition to live in! How warming
and vigorating to step into the brightness of this kind of love,
even for a few minutes.

> To look up and not down,
> To look forward and not back,
> To look out and not in,—
>   and
> To lend a hand.
>   EDWARD E. HALE

Everyone has an inner longing to feel important, to do
something unique, to have an assurance of his own worth.

Young people particularly have a terrible self-image. Their sense that they are not worth very much makes suicide rank high among the causes of adolescent death.

There's a preacher in New Jersey who has turned in his pulpit for a lunch counter across from the high school. For seven years he had been concerned about the people who never came inside his church. The first seven months after he bought the luncheonette, he made more contacts among teenagers than in the seven previous years.

He uses the interview technique at the counter, and carefully records each answer given him by a boy or girl. Then, during a conversation which arises around the significant questions he has asked, he hands his customer a little book. They usually read it and come back. They feel trusted.

Bill Iverson says, "Teen-agers want strong adult authority figures and adults who will listen to them, as well as acceptance by their peer group. They are crying for adults whom they can respect and who will tell them what to do at the right time. . . . Teenagers aren't asking for perfection—just honesty and integrity—what any adult ought to be able to give."

God has called us to be the expression of His love among the people of our own private world. If we can contain His kind of love that reaches out to others and holds no grudges, we will truly be light to brighten dark lives, for Christ's sake.

> The best way to destroy your enemy is to make him your friend.
>
> ABRAHAM LINCOLN

Dr. George W. Crane, author and social psychologist, has written a pamphlet called "The Compliment Club" (available from The Hopkins Syndicate, Mellot, Indiana). To qualify for membership in this club, a person undertakes to pay three sincere compliments a day, one to each of three different persons, for a month. He is encouraged to pay these to even casual contacts or complete strangers. The author points out that love cannot replace dislike or indifference at a moment's notice; it requires development of a definite technique, and of skill in approaching people.

Love grows through the showing of appreciation and dies without it. Christians ought to be the most skilled social detectives, ferreting out the good points in our associates. "You can sincerely compliment your worst enemy, for no human being is totally lacking in merits," says Crane.

> The art of praising is the beginning of the fine art of pleasing.

He tells many stories of how paying compliments changed people's lives. One woman working in a millinery house thought that Laura, who worked across the room from her, was snobbish and aloof. One day, however, to fill her quota of compliments, she said, "Laura, do you know that every time I glance up I see your head silhouetted against the window? I think you have the prettiest profile and hair of anyone I know."

Laura looked up startled, then began to cry. "That's the first kind word anybody has said to me in all the seventeen years I have worked here." All that time she had been hiding her loneliness from her co-workers behind a pseudo-sophistication.

"Friendship," says Crane, "is a flower. To obtain a lovely flower, somebody must do the work of planting the seed, watering and cultivating it."

Isn't this what Christ did? When He stopped to ask water from the Samaritan woman, when He told Zacchaeus He was going home to dinner with him, He was implying a compliment. He did somewhat the same thing with the despised publicans and sinners, even when He accepted the invitations of the Pharisees. What an important part of Christian love this is— to look for the good in people and help them to recognize it, to let them know that you believe good of them, rather than evil.

On a very intimate level we can gain another truth from this phrase about love. Love casts out the evil thinking that spoils our daydreams and our quiet times. Thoughts are the seeds to future deeds. God can not only cleanse the soul and heal the body, He can also purify the mind. Believers who would never dream of doing evil sometimes in their thinking wander down sordid paths. You become what you think.

> It is the thought of man . . . by which man works all things whatsoever. All that he does and brings to pass is the vesture of a thought.
>
> THOMAS CARLYLE

A young man, emerging from an evil place, accidentally met his pastor on the street. "I'm sorry," said the young man, "I had no business being there."

The wise pastor jolted the young man as he said, "When you came out and I saw you, you lost only your reputation. When you went in, and only God saw you, you lost your character."

Thousands of people have good reputations but have lost their characters. Omniscient God knows our thoughts completely.

Paul begs Christians to bring "into captivity every thought to the obedience of Christ" (2 Corinthians 10:5). Yes, God cleanses the mind as He pours in His love.

A university student approached me after a lecture and said, "I'm a Christian, but I'm up and down. My life is not consistent or constant." I made arrangements to meet him and further discuss his dilemma. When we met, I suggested going to his room. His definite reluctance was so obvious that I was sure my visit to his room would reveal his problem.

With his permission, we entered. I scanned the room with its pictures and books and immediately knew his trouble. Though upright in his conduct, the young man was filling his mind with the stories from pulp magazines and suggestive pictures. No wonder he was up and down in his experience! I counseled with him about his problem, and I am happy to say that after graduating from the university he went on to seminary, and today has his own pastorate.

The Scriptures can fill up the mind with life and hope. The love of Christ flows into the hungry places of our minds and souls and nourishes them abundantly. In this sense, too, love thinks no evil.

> Watch your thoughts, keep them strong;
> High resolve thinks no wrong.
> Watch your thoughts, keep them clear;
> Perfect love casts out fear.
> Watch your thoughts, keep them right;
> Faith and wisdom give you light.
> Watch your thoughts, keep them true;
> Look to God, He'll govern you.
>
> GRANVILLE KLEISER

It is interesting to notice that Paul tells the Philippians to think positively about wholesome virtues: "Whatever things are true, whatever things are honest, whatever things are just, whatever things are pure, whatever things are lovely, whatever things are of good report; if there be any virtue, and if there be any praise, think on these things" (Philippians 4:8). The phrase, "think on these things," suggests that we take an inventory of these things. Love notices and concentrates upon honesty, justice, purity, loveliness, and goodness, but not evil.

One man who began to allow God's love to come through in his daily contacts with people said, "I have found that the world is filled with interesting people. I just never realized it before." When the love of God leads us to see new values in others, we lose ourselves. And when we lose ourselves, as the Bible so paradoxically tells us, we finally begin to find ourselves!

All of this wonderful new kind of life is practical and possible only through the power of the indwelling Holy Spirit. The Holy Spirit loves spontaneously. With Him inside us, we begin to love as Christ loved. But He cannot work unless we allow Him to pour Himself through our thoughts and our actions.

Start with the first person you meet in the day. Is it your wife? your husband? the elevator operator? the bus driver? the paper boy? Maybe you are not in the habit of saying anything beyond a sort of unintelligible grunt. Look at this person in a whole new way—here is someone God's love can touch through you. Put yourself in the other person's shoes a minute, and see what comment you can make, what question you can phrase, that will make him feel good, make him know someone really cares.

On the other hand, if you don't really care, you can just go on using the same old recipe for a miserable life:

> Think about yourself.
> Talk about yourself.
> Use I as often as possible.
> Mirror yourself continually in the opinion of others.
> Listen greedily to what people say about you.
> Expect to be appreciated.
> Be suspicious.
> Be jealous and envious.
> Be sensitive to slights.
> Never forgive a criticism.
> Trust nobody but yourself.
> Insist on consideration and respect.
> Demand agreement with your own views on everything.
> Sulk if people are not grateful to you for favors shown them.
> Never forget a service you may have rendered.
> Be on the lookout for a good time for yourself.
> Shirk your duties if you can.
> Do as little as possible for others.
> Love yourself supremely.
> Be selfish.

This recipe is guaranteed to make one miserable! Love, on the contrary, never acts in any of these ways. Peter writes, "Seeing ye have purified your souls in obeying the truth through the Spirit unto unfeigned love of the brethren, see that ye love one another, with a pure heart fervently" (1 Peter 1:22).

SUGGESTED PRAYER

May Thy love be felt by others. Help us to speak the truth at all times in love. May we become more and more in every way like Christ who is the head of His body, the church. For in Christ, "The whole body fitly joined together and compacted by that which every joint supplieth . . . maketh increase of the body unto the edifying of itself in love (Ephesians 4:16). *Amen.*

REMINDERS

- Love does not behave in a discourteous manner. Greed does; selfishness does; fear does—but not love.

- "No man is an island, entire of itself, every man is a piece of the continent." JOHN DONNE

- In God's program, we stoop to conquer; we kneel to rise.

- When you lose control of yourself in any way, you really lose the ability to think and act as a rational human being.

- Love is optimistic; it looks at people in the best light. Love thinks constructively as it senses the grand possibilities in other people.

1 CORINTHIANS 13

If I [can] speak in the tongues of men and [even] of angels, but have not love [that reasoning, intentional, spiritual devotion such as is inspired by God's love for and in us], I am only a noisy gong or a clanging cymbal.

2 And if I have prophetic powers—that is, the gift of interpreting the divine will and purpose; and understand all the secret truths and mysteries and possess all knowledge, and if I have (sufficient) faith so that I can remove mountains, but have not love [God's love in me], I am nothing—a useless nobody.

3 Even if I dole out all that I have [to the poor in providing] food, and if I surrender my body to be burned [or in order that I may glory], but have not love [God's love in me], I gain nothing.

4 Love endures long and is patient and kind; love never is envious nor boils over with jealousy; is not boastful or vainglorious, does not display itself haughtily.

5 It is not conceited—arrogant and inflated with pride; it is not rude (unmannerly), and does not act unbecomingly. Love [God's love in us] does not insist on its own way, for it is not self-seeking; it is not touchy or fretful or resentful; it takes no account of the evil done to it—pays no attention to a suffered wrong.

6 It does not rejoice at injustice and unrighteousness, but rejoices when right and truth prevail.

7 Love bears up under anything and everything that comes, is ever ready to believe the best of every person, its hopes are fadeless under all circumstances and it endures everything [without weakening].

8 Love never fails—never fades out or becomes obsolete or comes to an end. As for prophecy [that is, the gift of interpreting the divine will and purpose], it will be fulfilled and pass away; as for tongues, they will be destroyed and cease; as for knowledge, it will pass away [that is, it will lose its value and be superseded by truth].

9 For our knowledge is fragmentary (incomplete and imperfect), and our prophecy (our teaching) is fragmentary (incomplete and imperfect).

10 But when the complete and perfect [total] comes, the incomplete and imperfect will vanish away—become antiquated, void and superseded.

11 When I was a child, I talked like a child, I thought like a child, I reasoned like a child; now that I have become a man, I am done with childish ways and have put them aside.

12 For now we are looking in a mirror that gives only a dim (blurred) reflection [of reality as in a riddle or enigma], but then [when perfection comes] we shall see in reality and face to face! Now I know in part (imperfectly); but then I shall know and understand fully and clearly, even in the same manner as I have been fully and clearly known and understood [by God].

13 And so faith, hope, love abide; [faith, conviction ana belief respecting man's relation to God and divine things; hope, joyful and confident expectation of eternal salvation; love, true affection for God and man, growing out of God's love for and in us], these three, but the greatest of these is love.

The Amplified New Testament (Grand Rapids: Zondervan, 1958) © The Lockman Foundation—1958. All rights reserved. Used by permission.

6

LOVE ONE ANOTHER

"Rejoiceth not in iniquity, but rejoiceth in the truth; Beareth all things, believeth all things, hopeth all things, endureth all things" (vv. 6-7).

People are little different today than they were in Christ's day. Human beings need to see and touch and feel in order to understand love. So God expressed His love centuries ago in a familiar form, one that could be seen and heard and experienced—Jesus Christ. Today He still requires people to be Christlike, so the modern world too can feel His love.

The church in the twentieth century is called to demonstrate the love of God in all its dealings with the world and its people. This way, even when the Scriptures are foreign, or obscure, or unavailable, God's people can be a universal language, "Known and read of all men" (2 Corinthians 3:2).

This is our highest calling as Christians. Here is the significance of the three little words taught in Sunday school that take a lifetime to practice: "Love one another."

In the heart of every individual is a primary hunger to love and to be loved. This can be fully satisfied only as a person comes into the total belonging he experiences as he receives Jesus Christ as Saviour and Lord.

Also within the soul of man is a contrary tendency which rejoices in the unloving characteristics of others. It is easy to see the mote in our brother's eye and ignore the beam in our own! We often seek to lift ourselves by pulling others down. Such is our deceitful nature.

79

Keep a fair-sized cemetery in your back yard, in
which to bury the faults of your friends.

HENRY WARD BEECHER

Love, on the contrary, refuses to capitalize on the shortcomings of others. Love implies caring—for better or for
worse. Love is an active concern for the life and growth of that
which we love. The very essence of love is to work for something and to help it grow. Love and labor are inseparable.

Search thy own heart, what paineth thee in others
in thyself may be.

JOHN GREENLEAF WHITTIER

You love what you work for, and you work hard for that
which you love. Love rejoices in the accomplishment of what
is honest and right.

"Rejoiceth not in iniquity" (v. 6).

On the negative side, love will not and cannot find satisfaction in that which is wrong. When you read that delinquency
is at an all-time high, what does it do to you? When you hear
about four boys bludgeoning a man to death, what do you feel
inside? When you read of an innocent girl attacked as she
sleeps, or a child kidnapped and brutally slain for money, what
is your reaction? When a thousand times a day, somewhere in
this country, a gavel drops and a judge says, "Divorce granted!"
does it bother you?

For evil to triumph, it is only necessary for good
men to do nothing.

EDMUND BURKE

To the Christian, sin is sad. Love cannot find any satisfaction in evil. But God's truth, as it is revealed in the growth of
those we love, those for whom we accept responsibility, is
great joy for the concerned Christian. When we see a delin-
quent boy brought into the shelter of such a place as Christian

Haven, or the Youth for Christ George Washington Home, and given a whole new life in Christ, it is cause for rejoicing. "Rejoice in the Lord always; and again I say, Rejoice" (Philippians 4:4).

If we are called to spend hours with a couple on the verge of divorce, and they somehow sense God's love in our concern and attention, and their old love is reborn and enriched by a new love for God, then we can sing and shout for joy. "Delight thyself also in the LORD; and he shall give thee the desires of thine heart" (Psalm 37:4).

It is often very helpful amid the problems of our age to ask the question, "What would our Lord do in this situation? How would Jesus act with this person, or this couple?" Jesus Christ was loving; He was also uncompromising. At times His words were so piercing that the people wanted to kill Him.

It is true that He went about doing good, but His goodness was firm and His words stringent, and He called forth the best in the people He met. He gave offense to His disciples, to His relatives, to the scribes and Pharisees, for He was always obedient to a higher loyalty. On one occasion, Jesus said, "Think not that I am come to send peace on earth; I came not to send peace, but a sword" (Matthew 10:34).

> The best way to show that a stick is crooked is not
> to argue about it or to spend time denouncing it,
> but to lay a straight stick along side it.
>
> D. L. MOODY

Jesus was loving and kind, but His kind of love is firm. When it came to evil, He was severe. God's love never rejoices in wrong but rejoices in the right.

"Beareth all things" (v. 7).

The word "beareth," used in this verse, literally means to cover, shelter, or protect. Love is a retreat which shelters people from the storms of life.

This pictorial word suggests placing a shield to shelter those underneath from danger. When a brother falls, what do you do? Do you lift him up, or cast him aside? Do you cover his faults, or whisper about them? Do you engage in character assassination, or do you try to work directly with the one in trouble? Unkind talk hinders the work of God a thousand times over. Critical tongues close church doors to hundreds of people. Unnecessary talk breaks the hearts and health of many pastors. Someone has said, "A critical tongue is like Samson's foxes with firebrands on their tails going among the cornstalks of the Philistines."

> The tongue is the only edged tool that grows keener
> with constant use.
>
> WASHINGTON IRVING

A person says, "Did you hear the awful story about Mr. So-and so? I was really sorry." He lies! He was glad, or else he would have kept it to himself. The gossip, the slanderer, is worse than the biggest thief in the world. The thief steals money, but the slanderer steals what money cannot buy—a man's reputation. A recognized weakness in someone else can make us feel superior as we talk about it, if we don't carefully ask for God's love in our reactions.

> The control of the tongue is the barometer of Christian maturity.

Our words can be more deadly than the poison of a snake. Paul says in Romans 3:13, "The poison of asps is under their lips." Common everyday griping and unnecessary criticism are poisons, in the Christian community and in our own souls.

Robert Burns, with great perception, writes about judging others:

> Who made the heart, 'tis He alone
> Decidedly can try us:

> He knows each chord, its various tone,
> Each spring, its various bias:
> Then at the balance let's be mute,
> We never can adjust it;
> What's done we partly may compute,
> But know not what's resisted.

Jesus said, "Judge not, that ye be not judged" (Matthew 7:1). When the scribes and Pharisees judged the woman caught in the act of adultery, Jesus turned and said, "He that is without sin among you, let him first cast a stone at her" (John 8:7). Jesus judged them for judging the woman. Those who judge others will receive God's judgment.

The Lord forgives and forgets, and so must we.

> God pardons like a mother, who kisses the offense
> into everlasting forgetfulness.
>
> HENRY WARD BEECHER

Love bears all things, believes all things, hopes all things, and endures all things.

A great aid in helping us accept the failures of others is remembering that God has covered all of our sins—sins of long ago and sins of today, sins of the body, of the soul, of the spirit, sins of omission and commission. The psalmist says: "As far as the east is from the west, so far hath he removed our transgressions from us" (Psalms 103:12). The prophet declared, "Thou wilt cast all their sins into the depths of the sea" (Micah 7:19). "I have blotted out, like a thick cloud, thy transgressions" (Isaiah 44:22). "Thou hast cast all my sins behind thy back" (Isaiah 38:17). He has not only forgiven but forgotten: "I will remember their sin no more" (Jeremiah 31:34). The Bible exhausts the possibility of language in telling us how God completely forgives.

> He who cannot forgive others breaks the bridge over
> which he must pass himself.
>
> GEORGE HERBERT

When Andrew Jackson was being questioned concerning church membership, the pastor asked, "General, there is one more question which I must ask you. Can you forgive all your enemies?" Andrew Jackson was silent as he recalled his stormy life of bitter fighting. Then he responded: "My political enemies I can freely forgive; but as for those who attacked me for serving my country, and those who slandered my wife—Doctor, I cannot forgive them!"

The pastor made it clear to Jackson that before he could become a member of that church and partake of the broken bread and the cup, his hatred and bitterness must be confessed and dealt with before God. Again there was an awkward silence, until Andrew Jackson affirmed that if God would help him, he would forgive his enemies.

There may be other occasions when we are called on to forgive our *friends*. Overreactions and underreactions on the part of people very dear to us sometimes result in unbearable situations which can tie us up in knots and drain our effectiveness. Whether the friend or relative is actually at fault matters little. Our response to his behavior can be quiet annoyance, or it can be the violent explosion of a burst of temper, a crying spell, a sudden withdrawal, a jealous act, or an unkind remark.

> He that is proud eats himself up; pride is his own
> mirror, his own trumpet, his own chronicle!
>
> WILLIAM SHAKESPEARE

A minister I know tells how he once was too proud to have any of the members of his congregation more spiritual than he was. One of the new members of this church was so in love with Christ that he couldn't stand her exhilarating influence in the congregation. First, he was upset after he had asked her to give the story of her conversion in the Sunday evening service— not because of her story, but because several people commented that it was the best service in months. It was hard for him to take because *he* had been preaching regularly at those other services!

Then he began to encounter such comments as, "Phyllis thinks it'd be a good idea," or "Phyllis suggested—" Then he found himself looking for ways to prove that Phyllis's ideas wouldn't work. He figured out ways to prove that she needed him. He looked for opportunities to show her that she really didn't know as much about spiritual things as she thought she did.

It was the new Christian in this case who asked for a confrontation. She said, bearing the conflict in love, "You are my pastor, and I need you. We seem to be fighting each other. We shouldn't do that. We're on the same side." She even asked his forgiveness for being hard to live with.

For two and a half hours they talked. The pastor found it humbling, even embarrassing. But this new convert helped him find himself. He was forgiven in a genuine outreach of love, and he in turn could ask for forgiveness in a pouring out of the competitive spirit and jealousy which had grounded his ministry.

What a release! Within a few months his whole congregation felt the new freedom. His sermons improved. Phyllis's spirit of love that bore his unjust combat enabled him finally to forgive and to profit from the bad feelings he had harbored.

> I will not permit any man to narrow and degrade my
> soul by making me hate him.
>
> BOOKER T. WASHINGTON

An unforgiving spirit blocks the forgiveness of God. A delicious sense of peace comes to the one who learns how to forgive. Love bears all that is placed upon its shoulders and covers all that is placed beneath its wings.

When you are tempted to gripe and complain about someone, remember the Scripture: "Be ye kind one to another, tenderhearted, forgiving one another, even as God for Christ's sake hath forgiven you" (Ephesians 4:32). What a measure of forgiving spirit!

"Believeth all things" (v. 7).

Love takes the kindest view possible of people and circumstances. Love searches for what is good and gives the benefit of the doubt.

A helpful prayer experiment began some years ago in Pittsburgh. A group of Christian businessmen saw very practical results of this expression of love—this believing in people—as they got under the burden with some men who were unemployed. As they became willing to spend time with these men who were out of jobs, they began to love them, to pray for them and with them.

One of the most interesting results of this communication of love through prayer lay in the response of the two hundred men who found employment during a nineteen-month period. It became apparent that most of them were finding their own jobs as this fellowship of love gave them increased confidence in themselves and renewed faith in God's personal concern for them. As a result of Christ's men believing in them, they were able to believe in themselves and move ahead.

One man said he left the first meeting and began to pray regularly that he would find a job. Sometime later, while preparing for his daily period of prayer, he stopped a moment and said to himself, "Mel, you've just been praying for work. Perhaps it's time to pray that the Lord will strengthen your faith." The next day the phone rang, and a man who had interviewed him some weeks before asked if he were still looking for employment. The very next day he went to work. Love has faith. Love trusts. Love believes in—inspires, lifts up.

The results in opening new doors to employment, in contacting people who were hiring around the city, were not coincidences. The men who were communicating God's love had no magic formula. But the results they could see were far beyond their limited human means.

"Hopeth all things" (v. 7).

Hope and great expectations are the antidotes for despair and gloom. For the most part, I am an optimist. People who are born with the kind of temperament that finds it easy to be sunny seem to have a bit of a head start in life.

> Optimism is the cheerful frame of mind that enables
> a teakettle to sing though in hot water up to its nose.
>
> ANONYMOUS

I am an optimist chiefly because I recognize that God is sovereign and His triumph is sure.

The psalmist sang, "I will bless the Lord at all times: his praise shall continually be in my mouth" (Psalm 34:1). David did not live a sheltered life. Saul hated him; Absalom rebelled against him; his baby died. Still his pattern of life was one of trust and hope. Love hopes in every conceivable experience. Love is optimistic, not pessimistic.

This is not a blind optimism, but a confidence based on God and His word. To the sinful, the Saviour said, "Be of good cheer; thy sins be forgiven thee" (Matthew 9:2). This is not empty sentimental talk; here is the most revolutionary statement a man can hear. There is hope for all who will turn to the Saviour for forgiveness. Nothing in all the world can cheer a person like the forgiveness of sin. "Blessed is he whose transgression is forgiven, whose sin is covered" (Psalm 32:1).

To the fearful, our Lord speaks: "Be of good cheer; it is I; be not afraid" (Matthew 14:27). These words were uttered to frightened men. Love is God's cure for fear. It shows up all the time—in our business procedures, our children's grades at school, our dating and marital practices, our attitude toward new assignments and new people. "There is no fear in love;

but perfect love casteth out fear: because fear hath torment. He that feareth is not made perfect in love" (1 John 4:18). Love opens up the heart, the mind, the hand, the purse. Fear clamps down on everything.

Some of our Christian efforts in the ghetto keep turning up evidence of what happens when young people come in contact with love that expects the best of them. Some who have floundered through school with Ds, demerits, and detentions, not caring one bit for the marks they were making, have literally come alive when they met Christ. For the first time they have found a reason for trying, a purpose in doing their best, and we have seen boys and girls straighten up and graduate from high school, instead of dropping out. One fellow said, "Before I met the Lord I had a D average going into my senior year. The school told me, 'You can quit.' But when I really heard how much Christ loved me, I prayed, 'Christ, if you're real, you better do something in my life, 'cause I need it.' I came back to school and made the honor roll at the end of my senior year, passed my college boards and they let me in college."

The terrified disciples, seeing a figure upon the waters, said, "It is a ghost" (Matthew 14:26), and cried out for fear. These experienced fishermen had passed through many storms, but they were not prepared for a spirit walking on the water. The unexplained experiences of life are always the most frightening, but God's presence gives abundant cause for hope. Love expects the best in everything.

"Endureth all things" (v. 7).

Love has an enduring quality. Through good times and bad times, through glad days and sad days, through doubt and darkness, love is persistent. It has the power to take it, even when it lacks the power to believe or hope. Love holds its ground.

You will not be carried to heaven lying at ease upon
a feather bed.

SAMUEL RUTHERFORD

Jeanie is a young, suburban high-school girl who met Christ
at a summer camp. This new love in her life has given her the
ability to look clearly at herself and her family. Her acceptance
of Jesus Christ as her personal Saviour did not remove the hard
things in her life, but it has given her fresh insights about them.
"My greatest fault," she says, "was cutting down kids. I never
even gave it a thought before. Now I can see how cruel this is.
When I start to rip someone apart now, I suddenly realize how
mean and selfish I am."

She also has a new attitude toward her father, a salesman
caught in the liquor routine. She used to avoid him and resent
him as a mean man. One of the first evidences of God's new
love flowing into Jeanie's life came almost immediately after
she said yes to Christ. "I wanted to get home right away," she
recalls. "I was afraid my mom was so lonely. I had always
taken her for granted, and, all of a sudden, I began to see that
my dad was really sick, not mean."

Jesus said, "In the world ye shall have tribulation; but be
of good cheer; I have overcome the world" (John 16:33).
Here is sufficient reason for optimism. Trials? Yes, but these
tribulations are merely opportunities to display God's power
and love. This enduring love is Godlike. Paul wrote to the
church at Corinth, "Love beareth all things, believeth all things,
hopeth all things, endureth all things" (v. 7).

Some time ago the area where we were living experienced a
terrible forest fire. The marks of the fierce blaze were thoroughly depressing. As I walked through the forest, I doubted
if anything had survived the inferno. All looked hopelessly
dead. Blackness prevailed. Six months later I went again and
witnessed a miracle. Nature, with a lush mantle of green, had

covered the darkness, overflowed the wounds, and hidden the scars. I walked in the midst of nature's profusion of goodness and prayed.

SUGGESTED PRAYER

Help me to live like this, Lord. Let the love of God flow through me to cover the shortcomings and the scars of life which make all of us difficult to love. Give me an understanding heart. Amen.

REMINDERS

• Love will not and cannot find satisfaction in that which is wrong.

• Love is a retreat which shelters people from the storms of life.

• "A critical tongue is like Samson's foxes with firebrands on their tails going among the cornstalks of the Philistines."

• "God pardons like a mother, who kisses the offense into everlasting forgetfulness." HENRY WARD BEECHER

• "I will not permit any man to narrow and degrade my soul by making me hate him." BOOKER T. WASHINGTON

• "He who cannot forgive others breaks the bridge over which he must pass himself." GEORGE HERBERT

• Optimism is the cheerful frame of mind that enables a teakettle to sing, though in hot water up to its nose.

1 CORINTHIANS 13

    I may speak with the tongues of man and of angels,
      but if I have no love,
        I am a noisy gong or a clanging cymbal;
2   I may prophesy, fathom all mysteries and secret lore,
    I may have such absolute faith that I can move hills from
      their place,
      but if I have no love,
        I count for nothing;
3   I may distribute all I possess in charity,
    I may give up my body to be burnt,
      but if I have no love,
        I make nothing of it.
4 Love is very patient, very kind. Love knows no jealousy; love
5 makes no parade, gives itself no airs, is never rude, never
6 selfish, never irritated, never resentful; love is never glad
7 when others go wrong, love is gladdened by goodness, always
   slow to expose, always eager to believe the best, always hope-
8 ful, always patient. Love never disappears. As for prophesying, it will be superseded; as for 'tongues,' they will cease;
9 as for knowledge, it will be superseded. For we only know bit
10 by bit, and we only prophesy bit by bit; but when the perfect
11 comes, the imperfect will be superseded. When I was a child,
   I talked like a child, I thought like a child, I argued like a child;
   now that I am a man, I am done with childish ways.
12   At present we only see the baffling reflections in a mirror,
      but then it will be face to face;
    at present I am learning bit by bit,
      but then I shall understand, as all along I have myself been
        understood.
13 Thus 'faith and hope and love last on, these three,' but the
   greatest of all is love.

The New Testament: A New Translation by James Moffatt (New York: Harper & Row, 1922). Used by permission.

7

LOVE NEVER FAILS

"Love never faileth" (v. 8).

We live in an exploding age. Man has split and fused the atom, placing tremendous energy at his disposal. He has attained speeds of travel unknown to any other generation.

In 1927 Charles Lindberg crossed the Atlantic, flying at a speed of about one hundred miles an hour and an altitude of five thousand feet. Today our jet aircraft fly more than two thousand miles per hour at eighty thousand feet. A supersonic trip between New York and Paris is now less than a three-hour ride. Serious study is being given to hypersonic transport, which deals with speeds up to seven thousand miles per hour.

United Airlines estimates that by 1990, rockets will be sufficiently developed for commercial transportation, so that we can blast off from Chicago and make a soft landing in Manila—17,000 miles away—in about forty-five minutes. Stupendous, isn't it? We have seen more material changes in the last one hundred years than in all recorded history. And yet, despite all of this technological advancement, we still have not discovered how to live together in harmony.

> We can fly like the bird,
> And swim like the fish,
> If we could only learn
> To behave like men—we'd
> Be doing something.
> VANCE HAVNER

93

Lillian Smith, late author and outspoken champion of racial equality, talked about how the twentieth century is becoming the age of human relations. Suddenly we are only a few hours from everyone on earth, and we can share answers to temporal conflict.

At the same time, modern technology has given us new instruments and insights with which we can examine and understand ourselves. "It has crept upon us so quietly," she wrote in *The Journey,* "we have hardly noticed. But it is one of the significant events of the twentieth century: these groups of men and women, finding their tongues, sloughing off the old mutism and doing it just as science gives them the means of world-wide communication. Not arguing, not debating, not defending and entrenching their past mistakes. Not on trial. Simply saying, 'It was this way with me.' "

Too often we have not provided opportunity for people to express how it is with them. The church is a classic example of a situation where we can get together with four hundred or four thousand people on Sunday morning and yet not really know anyone. We can participate in a significant worship service, without ever really getting to know the person sitting with us in the pew

> To love the whole world
> For me is no chore;
> My only real problem's
> My neighbor next door.
> C. W. VANDERBERGH

A minister in the pastoral care department of one of Chicago's newest hospitals feels that the Christian church today has a tremendous potential which has not been tapped. "Our churches are worship-centered," says Larry Holst, "and project-centered, but not person-centered. . . . Christian fellowship is coming to see ourselves as we are—the splendor and the grandeur of man created in the image of God, as well as his misery, the potential of man in Christ, as well as his sinfulness. If we could get our congregations to be sensitive to the inter-personal feelings and relationships that are so crucial to people, I think we could turn many of our 'sleeping giants' into powerhouses of God's healing love."

> Love is friendship set on fire.
> JEREMY TAYLOR

The thing that most often causes people to collapse is the absence of a demonstration of God's love to one another.

> We will win the world when we realize that fellowship, not evangelism, must be our primary emphasis. When we demonstrate the Big Miracle of Love, it won't be necessary for us to go out—they will come in.
> JESS MOODY

The infant church in the book of Acts was a warmhearted, spirit-filled, loving fellowship.

> People don't go where the action is, they go where love is.
> JESS MOODY

The ancient sophist used to say, "Nothing will last." In direct contrast, Paul announces, love will last.

EARTHLY THINGS FAIL

Yes, earthly things fail. The word "fail" has two technical meanings. The classical Greek presents the picture of a bad actor being hissed off the stage. Of course, love is not like this, as it lives on even on the stage of eternity. Love is never hissed off the stage. The other picture is of a fading flower with falling petals. Love never withers, fades, nor falls away. Love never loses its place.

Paul spoke about unusual spiritual gifts—the gift of prophecy, the ability to speak, and knowledge. These God-given gifts, he said, would terminate, but love lasts. Love is the most enduring virtue in our world.

> The desire of power in excess caused the angels to fall; the desire of knowledge in excess caused man to fall, but in love there is no excess, neither can angel or man come in danger by it.
>
> BACON

When we wish to speak of lasting things, we speak of the everlasting hills and the unchanging heavens, but even these symbols of permanency undergo change. All about us we see the elements wasting under the powers of corruption. Giant trees, once monarchs of the forest, are now bent and broken with age. All nature groans under this process of death.

The Bible says, "All the hills shall melt" (Amos 9:13). As to the unchanging heavens, we read, "As a vesture shalt thou fold them up, and they shall be changed" (Hebrews 1:12). Let's remember, "The things which are seen are temporal; but the things which are not seen are eternal" (2 Corinthians 4:18).

Where are the lavish, exotic hanging gardens of Babylon? They are all gone. Where are the majestic temples of Greece? For the most part, they are broken memories of the golden age. The great empires of yesterday have been led to the tomb by the hand of time.

> We live in the kind of a world in which the only constant factor is change, and some of the changes are unhappy ones. . . . What do we do when the roof falls in?
>
> EILEEN GUNDER

Death uproots and pulls down all creation. Every field has a grave, every city a cemetery. This ugly invader not only turns creation's beauty to ashes, but brings the creature to dust. Death darkens the eyes of those we love; it eventually shakes our own limbs and shuts the door on this life. Mortality reigns in our bodies. Death starts at birth. Earthly things fail.

In complete contrast, love is eternal. Though everything else is mortal, love is immortal. When all else fails, love never fails. An accurate translation could be, "Love never falls down on the job." It not only never fails, it never ends. Even when the roof of life caves in, love abides.

> Love is the best thing in the world, and the thing that lives longest.
>
> VAN DYKE

Jealousy over spiritual gifts had gripped the Corinthian Christians. This is probably why Paul stressed that the greatest gift is love for each member of the body of Christ, no matter how unimportant he might seem. Love was for the Corinthians; love is for you, too.

The history of the world has been one of greed, selfishness and war, rather than of love. Emerson, in *Man, The Reformer,* said, "Love would put a new face on this weary old world in which we dwell as pagans and enemies too long, and it would warm the heart to see how fast the vain diplomacy of statesmen, the impotence of armies, and navies, and lines of defence, would be superseded by this unarmed child. Love will creep where it cannot go, will accomplish that by imperceptible methods—being its own lever, fulcrum, and power—which force could never achieve."

Love is powerful beyond our imagination. Jesus Christ demonstrated this power in His life and in His death. The cross is a great illustration of the conquering force of God's love.

JESUS NEVER FAILS

Since Jesus is the fulfillment of every characteristic listed in 1 Corinthians 13, it would be absolutely right to say that Jesus never fails.

In reality, just about everything in this life fails. Fame fails. The world, writes John, passes away. Sometimes business fails. Governments fail. Friends often let us down. Health fails. Yes, everything fails except that which is centered in Christ. "Christ in you, the hope of glory" (Colossians 1:27).

The apostle Peter failed Jesus. He followed afar off and denied Christ on three successive opportunities. He said he would die with Him, yet he openly denied Christ.

Thomas failed. When the disciples spoke of the resurrection, he doubted and said, "Except I shall see in his hands the prints of the nails, and put my finger into the print of the nails, and thrust my hand into his side, I will not believe" (John 20:25).

The disciples failed. After Jesus' Gethsemane experience, "The disciples forsook him, and fled" (Matthew 26:56). They let Him down. When Jesus was on the cross, they cried, "come down." It would have been very human for Him to come down, but it was divine for Him to hang there. The love that God gives to you and me builds trust and faithfulness even when the roof caves in.

It is comforting to know that the failure of the disciples did not alter Christ's love for them. Eventually Peter wept bitterly at his coolness. Thomas cried out, "My Lord and my God" (John 20:28). The disciples came back for cleansing and restoration. We in the twentieth century fail Him too, but Jesus never fails, for He is God. His love is eternal. The most exciting adventure in life is to be controlled by God's love, for then all that we do will be eternal. The command He has given us is: "These things I command you, that ye love one another" (John 15:17).

> Life is not as idle ore
>   But iron dug from central gloom,
> And heated hot with burning fears,
>   And dipt in baths of hissing tears,

And battered with the shocks of doom
To shape and use.

TENNYSON

LOVE IS ETERNAL

Millions of people viewed Michelangelo's famous Pieta when it was on exhibit at the New York World's Fair. It is a sculpture of the crucified Christ in the arms of Mary. It has been called marble in rhythm. Someday this masterpiece will crumble and the name of its creator will be forgotten. But a deed which is done in love will last forever. To be motivated by God's love is to live with eternity's values in view. The great paintings of the masters will all pass into oblivion, but our acts of love will abide. Love never ends.

Recently I visited the 110-story, 1454-foot Sears Tower, the tallest man-made structure on earth. It is a fantastic architectural feat, but someday its tons of concrete will be broken and its designer's name will be forgotten. And yet a cup of cold water, given in love, will break upon the shores of eternity. In a world gone mad with greed and hate, how wonderful to know that love never dies. Love is never obsolete. Love never fails.

Because of this truth, let us pray daily for this gift of love. When we come to the close of this life, the majority of us will say, "We did not love enough." May we experience the greatest marvel of all time, the greatest realization of ourselves. Let us humbly seek the openness in our lives that enables our family and friends to feel loved by us, and to say in wonder, "God is here!"

SUGGESTED PRAYER

I thank Thee for the abiding power of love. May we look beyond the troubles all around us, forward to the joys of heaven which we have not yet seen. Our

troubles will soon go away, but the joys to come will
last forever. Amen.

REMINDERS

- "Love is friendship set on fire." JEREMY TAYLOR

- "Love will creep where it cannot go, will accomplish that by imperceptible methods,—being its own lever, fulcrum, and power,—which force could never achieve." EMERSON

- Since Jesus is the fulfillment of every characteristic listed in 1 Corinthians 13, it would be absolutely right to say that Jesus never fails.

- To be motivated by God's love is to live with eternity's values in view.

- The most exciting adventure in life is to be controlled by God's love, for then all that we do will be eternal.

1 CORINTHIANS 13

If I can speak with the tongues of men and of angels, but have not love, I am a blaring trumpet or a clanging cymbal. Or if I can prophesy and am versed in all mysteries and all 2 knowledge, and have such absolute faith that I can remove mountains, but have not love, I am nothing. And if I use all 3 I have to feed the poor, and give up my body to be burned, but have not love, it profits me nothing.

Love is forbearing and kind. Love knows no jealousy. Love 4 does not brag; is not conceited. She is not unmannerly, nor 5 selfish, nor irritable, nor mindful of wrongs. She does not 6 rejoice in injustice, but joyfully sides with the truth. She can 7 overlook faults. She is full of trust, full of hope, full of endurance.

Love never fails. But if there are prophecies, they will come 8 to an end; if there are tongues, they will cease; if there is knowledge, it will come to an end. For our knowledge is par- 9 tial, and so is our prophesying; but when that which is perfect 10 is come, all that is partial will come to an end. When I was a 11 child, I talked like a child, thought like a child, reasoned like a child; now that I have become a man, I have put an end to childish ways. For at present we see things as in a mirror, 12 obscurely; but then we shall see face to face. At present I gain but partial knowledge, but then I shall know fully, even as I am fully known. And so there remain faith, hope, love— 13 these three; but of these the greatest is love.

The New Testament in Modern Speech by Richard Weymouth, 6th ed. (New York: Harper & Bros., n.d.). Used by permission of Harper & Row, Publishers, Inc.

8

HOW TO LOVE

"And hope maketh not ashamed, because the love of God is shed abroad in our hearts by the Holy Spirit who is given unto us" (Romans 5:5).

The apostle Paul begins 1 Corinthians 13 by stating that without love, "I am nothing." Nothing is the opposite of something. The apostle bluntly tells us here that it is love or nothing.

There are many stories of the miraculous changes that occur in people's lives when they experience God's love. Love is really the aliveness of God's Holy Spirit in us. We cannot have one without the other. What life is to the physical body, the Holy Spirit is to our spiritual nature.

> The Holy Spirit is God at work.
>
> D. L. MOODY

A group of former narcotic addicts is saying the same thing in the twentieth century. On heroin from four to sixteen years, they came to Jesus Christ because they had tried everything else and had found no way out. John Giminez of New York City describes the experience of delivery from drugs through the gift of the Holy Spirit:

> God brings His Holy Spirit into messed up humans. That bursting forth of the Spirit within us is so peaceful and beautiful and sweet! We struggled so hard for so long to keep our bodies satisfied, and suddenly here was this won-

103

derful Holy Spirit satisfying both our flesh and our spirit.
. . . When we come home to God we get loved like we never
have been loved before by anyone. We can walk with our
heads up and smiles on our faces. . . .

Since we discovered that God really loves us, and it
doesn't matter any more all the terrible things we have
done, then we can try to help other people make the same
discovery we made. . . . We know what it feels like to be
lost. But we know now what it feels like to come home.
We can see all the wonderful possibilities in a person. In
a girls' prison, for instance, we can tell them, "God loves
and cares for you." We can see ahead what God has for
them when they come to Him. They can be fit mothers and
loving wives. We know that God can do this for them because He has done so much for us.

Let me share steps in learning how to love.

STEP ONE

The source of all love is God. This is where love comes
from, for "God is love" (1 John 4:8). Let us go back to the
very beginning. The very first step is to receive Jesus Christ
as your Saviour. He is God's gift of love to you. Without this
salvation experience, you will find everything else impossible.
Jesus said, "Except a man be born again, he cannot see the
kingdom of God" (John 3:3).

> One might better try to sail the Atlantic in a paper
> boat, than to get to heaven on good works.
>
> CHARLES H. SPURGEON

Many people are trying to find self-respect and the respect
of others rather than what they really need—God's salvation.
We need first of all to face the fact that we are not whole; we
are not well; we are not capable of making it by ourselves.
Sin is missing the mark of God's standard, and we all fit that
description. It is willful disobedience, or lack of obedience to
God's written Word and to the living Word, Jesus Christ. The

Scriptures remind us, "All the world [is] guilty before God" (Romans 3:19).

The recognition of sin is the beginning of salvation.

ANONYMOUS

When we understand that Christ is God's remedy, that God—in His love—made this whole magnificent arrangement so that we can be complete as a person, then we will want to ask His forgiveness for our sin. "But as many as received him, to them gave he power to become the children of God, even to them that believe on his name" (John 1:12). We believe God, receive His answer to our dilemma, and we become children of God! That's what He said—children of God!

To know anything about the love of God, one must truly know God. Love is not a law or a code, but a Person. This is one of the most remarkable things about the Christian faith. God knew we could not love until we had felt it, experienced it. So He expressed His love in a human form—Jesus Christ—so we human beings could grasp the patience, the kindness, the humbleness, the confidence, the optimism, the joy that is contained in His perfect love.

The important question, then, is this: Do you know Jesus Christ? Have you invited Him into your life to be the power that will make you a new person—a child of God?

STEP TWO

In order to understand how to love, you must experience the power of God's love in your life. Paul told the believers at Rome, "The love of God is shed abroad in our hearts by the Holy Spirit who is given unto us" (Romans 5:5).

Many people make the mistake of struggling to get the fruits of the Spirit without ever yielding themselves to the Holy Spirit Himself. This kind of effort is a waste of time. *The secret of the fullness of love is the fullness of the Holy Spirit.*

The Scripture plainly teaches that when we receive Jesus

Christ as Saviour we actually become the dwelling place of the Holy Spirit. This is a staggering truth! Think of it—God the Holy Spirit, living in us all the time!

Paul put it this way, "Know ye not that ye are the temple of God, and that the Spirit of God dwelleth in you?" (1 Corinthians 3:16).

In times past, God was in the tabernacle and then in the temple. But where is He now? The Bible says, "Christ in you, the hope of glory" (Colossians 1:27). The moment you receive Christ, the Holy Spirit comes to live in your body.

The word "dwell" used in 1 Corinthians 3:16 has a beautiful depth of meaning. It means to settle down to stay, permanently, as we do in our own homes. The Holy Spirit is a personal, permanent guest. The Holy Spirit is God in us *all the time.*

But He is not there just to be taken for granted. The Holy Spirit may be grieved because of our carelessness. Paul warns, "Grieve not the holy Spirit of God, whereby ye are sealed unto the day of redemption" (Ephesians 4:30). The word "grieve" means to cause sorrow. G. Campbell Morgan asked, "How would you like to be compelled to live with somebody who was everlastingly grieving your heart by his conduct?" How terrible we feel when we hurt someone we love! We would do *anything* to make amends for the disappointment, the heartbreak we have caused the beloved. Let us not grieve or quench the indwelling Holy Spirit. He is the source of love in us. May we rather "Be filled with the Spirit" (Ephesians 5:18).

> I believe that the moment our hearts are emptied of pride, self-seeking, and all that is contrary to God's Word, the Holy Spirit will fill every corner of our hearts.
>
> D. L. MOODY

"But how can I do this?" you ask. The fullness of the Spirit is dependent upon your yieldedness. When you want God's will in your life, you will think, talk, walk, and live in this desire. This is the happy relationship of love. "It is not *my* love," you will say, "but *His* love; not *my* ability, but *His* ability in me."

Under normal and natural human conditions, you are not inclined to sacrifice and suffer for others, but when you are dominated by the Holy Spirit, love and sacrifice spring spontaneously to your mind and heart. You begin to see people in new ways. You recognize selfishness in yourself and needs in others, that you never saw before. The natural man loves the praise of the people all around him, while the Spirit-filled person yearns for the praise of God. To know real fullness of love you must allow a change in your heart, a change of focus from self to Christ. This change comes from placing God's Holy Spirit in the driver's seat of your life. It results in God's love working *in* you, and out to others *through* you.

Just as you accepted new life by faith in Christ, you are to accept by faith the fullness of the Spirit which He promises us. Paul, writing to the Galatians, states "Receive the promise of the Spirit through faith" (3:14). "Through faith" places this gift within the reach of each believer. The youngest Christian can understand this and know this fullness of love. Do not look at yourself and your shortcomings and get depressed and bogged down.

> Faith, like light, should always be simple and unbending; while love, like warmth, should beam forth on every side, and bend to every necessity of our brethren.
>
> MARTIN LUTHER

The disciples could see the hopelessness of living a life of love in their own strength. They knew it was impossible, and so do you. But the great good news is just this: God knew it too! Look at Jesus Christ and His faithfulness. God's perfect character stands behind His promises. His perfect love will fill us if we let it Don't struggle—*believe!*

STEP THREE

Seek the fruit of the Spirit. Paul says, "The fruit of the Spirit is love" (Galatians 5:22). Don't get worried and impatient with God's timing. Fruit comes slowly. Remember that it takes a seed, a flower, pollenization, warm sunshine, cold rains, and contrary winds to produce the finished fruit. That's true in life, too. Our lives are made up of sunshine and rain, blue skies and black, harsh winds and pruning shears. All of these work to produce this precious fruit called love.

Are you yielding to the Holy Spirit? Do you know what it is to demonstrate love? All other gifts you may possess are less important than this fruit of the Holy Spirit. Let this love that comes from God be plentiful in our lives. The ninefold fruit of the Spirit is the reproduction of the life and love of Jesus Christ in us.

In counseling with young people all over the world, I have observed that the primary goals they are seeking are love, joy, and peace. These are the three greatest pursuits. Isn't it interesting that the Bible tells us in Galatians 5:22 that "the fruit of the Spirit is love, joy, peace." The goals of our young people can be realized by experiencing the fruit of the Holy Spirit.

STEP FOUR

Pray for an abounding love. Paul writes, "And this I pray, that your love may abound yet more and more in knowledge and in all judgment" (Philippians 1:9). The word "abound" suggests the sea waves as they roll in, overflowing in every direction. This is love that gives freely of itself without seeking anything in return. We are told to *pray* for this kind of love. In other words, make love your aim.

A little girl was busily playing with her dolls when suddenly she left them and climbed upon her mother's lap to hug and kiss her affectionately. The surprised mother asked, "Why did you leave your dolls and come to Mother?" The simple, childish answer was, "Mother, I love my dolls, but my dollies never love me back."

How important it is to be loved! God has given each one of us a free will. We are not mechanical robots. How wonderful it is to tell the Lord that we love Him. Even with all our faults we can, so to speak, climb on His lap and express our love. There is nothing that gives Him greater joy than our childlike response to His magnificent love. We need to pray earnestly each day that God's abounding love might shine forth from our lives.

STEP FIVE

Begin to love by faith. Believe God for the love you cannot muster in yourself. Say, "Lord, by faith I *will* love that unlovable person."

Some people, because of past actions, are extremely difficult to love. Recently, a twenty-two-year-old young lady came to me for counsel. As we talked, she poured out a story of hate and bitterness that centered in her parents.

After sharing with her from God's Word, I was able to lead her to accept Christ as her personal Saviour. Almost immediately she said, "I want to be reconciled with my parents, but how can I love them?"

"By faith," I replied. "Go home and believe that God will give you a new love for your mother and father. He can and He will!"

D. L. Moody relates this incident in his life:

> One day in New York, oh, what a day, I cannot describe it, I seldom refer to it, it is almost too sacred an experience to name; I can only say God revealed Himself to me. I had such an experience of His love that I had to ask Him to stay His hand. I went to preaching again; the sermons were no different, I did not present any new truth,

yet hundreds were converted, and I would not be placed back where I was before that blessed experience if you would give me all Glasgow.

Moody had such a great hunger and thirst after God's fullness that he had searched—yes, even pleaded—for God to fill him. Do you really hunger and thirst for this love?

How shall I love? Think of someone who gets on your nerves. Pray for that one. Ask God specifically to bless him. Remember it was when Job prayed for his miserable comforters that he was released from his own captivity.

Prayer has a boomerang effect. Prayer benefits the one who prays. Perhaps you will want to make a list of that person's good qualities and even his bad qualities. You might then ask why the person has those bad qualities. Then, in an act of genuine faith, resolve to love that person.

I have seen thousands of people learn how to love by taking these five basic steps. Will you learn how to love?

In our world, love shows itself by action. Our Lord said, "Ye shall know them by their fruits" (Matthew 7:16). This means that our service, our behavior, will be a test of our love for Christ.

Obedience is the fruit of faith.

CHRISTINA ROSETTI

But Jesus went even further when He said, "Not every one that saith unto me, Lord, Lord, shall enter into the kingdom of heaven; but he that doeth the will of my Father, who is in heaven" (Matthew 7:21). And again He said, "If ye love me, keep my commandments" (John 14:15). "He that hath my commandments, and keepeth them, he it is that loveth me" (v. 21). "By this shall all men know that ye are my disciples, if ye have love one to another" (John 13:35). It is all very plain. We can hardly mistake His meaning.

It is a great deal easier to do that which God gives

us to do, no matter how hard it is, than to face the
responsibilities of not doing it.

J. R. MILLER

What is the proof of love? Love itself. One day the risen
Christ talked with Simon Peter, the denier, with this question,
"Simon, son of Jonah, lovest thou me more than these?" (John
21:15). When Peter answered, "Yea, Lord," the Saviour said,
"Feed my lambs." Jesus repeated the same question, and Peter
gave the same answer. Then the Saviour said, "Feed my sheep"
(v. 16). Jesus questioned Simon the third time (as many
times as Peter had denied Christ). At this continued pressing,
the Scripture tells us, "Peter was grieved, . . . And he said unto
him, Lord, thou knowest all things; thou knowest that I love
thee. Jesus saith unto him, Feed my sheep" (v. 17). Jesus was
emphasizing the necessary relationship between *loving* and
feeding the sheep.

Service can never become slavery to one who loves.

J. L. MASSE

Real love always serves. It lasts Love is not content to sit
and do nothing. Love is active. It has to express itself in giving, in serving, in being. The proof of our love comes in our
ability and our willingness to help other people. The high-
school girl who used to "cut down" people, now sees the selfishness in this practice. She has a God-given desire to understand
the shortcomings of her friends—as well as her own. She wants
to pray for them and help them understand themselves. The
woman who had heard rumors about the two women who lived
alone found that the love of God overcame her concern, her
fear, so that she was able to share abroad the love of Christ in
a home that had literally fallen apart without love.

Only a burdened heart can lead to fruitful service.

ALAN REDPATH

One woman who was at her wit's end tells of this experience.

During a long winter, sickness and accident had struck just about everyone in her family. Mumps, measles, a broken nose, a broken leg, and four new teeth for the baby made pressures and demands accumulate till she fell on her knees to protest in desperation, "Oh, Lord! I have so much to do!" To her astonishment, what came out was quite different. The words she heard herself cry out instead were these: "Oh, Lord! I have so much to *love!"*

What a difference there is in life when we can transpose those two little words. How many ways we can find to express that love: planting hope where there is no hope; listening to the cry of a rebellious teenager; soothing the pain of a hospital patient; giving cool water to a dying enemy on the battlefield; visiting the shut-in; helping the widow; taking in the orphan; and ministering to the man in prison.

We can leave a pot of soup for the woman just out of the hospital, collect money to help an elderly couple whose home was burned; share a flower with someone who is sad, help a blind person to a chair in the station, cuddle a lost child, share breakfast with a man on skid row. We can counsel high-school people at a summer camp, discuss our own experience of God's love with the neighbor child who comes to chat, talk with the woman next door, invite the man in our office to go fishing with us.

There are countless ways in which the Holy Spirit will ask us to love, as we yield our seconds, our minutes, our days to Him—as we hold up our friendships, our difficult relationships, our families, our encounters with strangers to Him.

Love cannot sit still and do nothing. It will eagerly look for the day when the King of love will come in person, but it has to be demonstrating His love to love-starved people while it looks.

Love is action, and the proof of your love for Jesus Christ will be found in your service to others. The nurse's aide in the hospital who gently washes the hands, the legs, the feet of the man dying of cancer, is getting very close to the example of

Christ as He washed His disciples' feet. "As ye have done it unto one of . . . these . . . ye have done it unto me" (Matthew 25:40).

I do not mean by all this that we must always be on the go. Surely we must worship before we work; meditation must precede ministering; being tuned in to the Spirit precedes being tuned in to others. There must always be that retirement in which our soul is prepared for action.

We have become a meeting-oriented people. We go, go, go. Arnold Toynbee, in his *Study of History*, writes of history being composed of "a moment of withdrawal." To serve without preparation is to thoroughly exhaust oneself. When the crowds sought to make Jesus king, He departed into His mountain retreat. Before He began His public ministry, He spent forty days in the wilderness. Our Lord practiced moments of withdrawal.

The early Christians gave themselves to prayer and communion, which in turn resulted in service. How much more do we in this jet age need to worship Christ before we can work for Christ? "They that wait upon the Lord shall renew their strength, they shall mount up with wings like eagles; they shall run, and not be weary; and they shall walk, and not faint" (Isaiah 40:31).

Mary chose to sit at the feet of Jesus while Martha served. When you are yielded to the Holy Spirit, your worship and work will be blended together. Service is the fruit of worship. The fullness of love comes only through the fullness of the Holy Spirit.

SUGGESTED PRAYER

More than anything in life we want fullness of love. In childlike faith we yield ourselves completely to the indwelling Holy Spirit. Shed Thy love abroad in our hearts. In simple faith we claim and accept the fullness of love. Amen.

REMINDERS

• The source of all love is God. This is where love comes from, for "God is love" (1 John 4:8).

• Five steps in knowing how to love:
    1. Receive Christ as your Saviour. He is God's gift of love to you.
    2. Experience the power of God's love in your life. "The love of God is shed abroad in our hearts" (Romans 5:5).
    3. Seek the fruit of the Spirit.
    4. Pray for an abounding love.
    5. Begin to love by faith. Believe God for the love you cannot muster in yourself.

• "Service can never become slavery to one who loves." J. L. MASSE

1 CORINTHIANS 13

1 Though I speak with the tongues of men and of angels, and have not love, I am become as sounding bronze, or a tinkling cymbal.

2 And though I have the gift of prophecy, and understand all mysteries, and all knowledge; and though I have all faith so that I could remove mountains, and have not love, I am nothing.

3 And though I bestow all my goods to feed the poor, and though I give my body to be burned, and have not love, it profiteth me nothing.

4 Love suffereth long, and is kind; love envieth not; love vaunteth not itself, is not puffed up,

5 Doth not behave itself unseemly, seeketh not its own, is not easily provoked, thinketh no evil,

6 Rejoiceth not in iniquity, but rejoiceth in the truth;

7 Beareth all things, believeth all things, hopeth all things, endureth all things.

8 Love never faileth; but whether there be prophecies, they shall be done away; whether there be tongues, they shall cease; whether there be knowledge, it shall vanish away.

9 For we know in part, and we prophesy in part.

10 But when that which is perfect is come, then that which is in part shall be done away.

11 When I was a child, I spoke as a child, I understood as a child, I thought as a child; but when I became a man, I put away childish things.

12 For now we see in a mirror, darkly; but then, face to face; now I know in part, but then shall I know even as also I am known.

13 And now abideth faith, hope, love, these three; but the greatest of these is love.

The New Scofield Reference Bible, ed. C. I. Scofield (New York: Oxford U., 1967). Reprinted by permission.

9

THE FOUNDATION OF LOVE

"A new commandment I give unto you, that ye love one another; as I have loved you, that ye also love one another" (John 13:34).

A popular tune of a few years ago suggested that *love* is the answer to the world's great needs. "What the world needs now is love, sweet love," says the songwriter. "It's the only thing that there's just too little of." With that sentiment we certainly agree.

But no matter how many words are written, no matter how songs are sung, we still see very little genuine love in this cold and impersonal world.

The apostle Paul tells us that there are many things in life that are important, but the most important of all is God's love. His love is the foundation of all that is worthwhile. It is the supreme ingredient of living. Paul reminds us that all other gifts, minus love, equals zero.

LOVE IS THE FOUNDATION OF THE FAMILY

Love for each member of the family is the basis of the home, and a picture of God's relationship with his children. A lack of love in the home brings nearly three quarters of a million couples into the divorce courts of America in an average year. Jesus explained that Moses permitted a man to divorce his wife because he recognized the hardness and lovelessness of the human heart. "It was not what God originally intended," He told His disciples. (See Matthew 19:3-8.)

117

Success in marriage consists not only in finding the
right mate, but also in being the right mate.

ANONYMOUS

With the many modern pressures that now bear down upon
the average home, it is questionable whether a family can stay
together without a firm foundation in selfless love.

The family is the school of duties . . . founded on
love.

FELIX ADLER

Jesus told a story about a home built upon the sand and
another built upon a rock (Matthew 7:24-27). When the
storm came, the home built upon the sand fell. Today there are
too many homes built upon the sand.

Paul instructed the Colossians, "Wives, submit yourselves
unto your own husbands. . . . Husbands, love your wives"
(3:18-19).

Just as Jesus Christ loved and sacrificed for the church, so
the husband is to love the wife. The florists tell us to "say it
with flowers." That's a fine suggestion, isn't it? Another suggestion is to say it *with words*. Why not call up a loved one
and express in words all that they mean to you?

The best way to compliment your wife is frequently.

For example, a husband could phone his wife and say, "Dar-
ling, I've called just to say I love you, and when I got you I hit
the jackpot." Undoubtedly she'll be shocked, but also very
pleased. And when you arrive home, I wouldn't be surprised if
you were served the best meal you've enjoyed in a long time.
Even though the dinner is not your goal, I do not know where
you can get so much for so little. Let's begin to express our
love verbally.

The art of praising is the beginning of the fine art of
pleasing.

When Jesus wanted to let people see something of God's love, He told the story of the prodigal son returning home after squandering everything. While the repentant boy was still a long way from home, the loving father saw him and ran to welcome him back. Never forget that the eyes of love are swifter than the feet of repentance. Instead of rebuking the son, the father hugged and kissed him and then celebrated the occasion with a lavish party.

We need to tell our children often of our deep love for them. The cords of love will keep open the lines of communication even when there is a lack of understanding.

Perhaps right now you are having a conflict with your parents. Though it may sound overly simplistic, love is the solution to that problem. Approach the problem carefully and prayerfully.

First, carefully write out the offenses of your parents. This is helpful, as it will identify your area of difficulty. It will also help you remove the hostility from your system.

Second, list your own deficiencies. At first you may not be aware of your offenses, but think carefully—because you are part of the problem. How are your attitudes? Do you ever express thankfulness? How do you respond to authority? Why not put yourself in their place? Relive the problem through their eyes.

Then in faith, lovingly seek reconciliation and harmony. Ask God to give you open lines of communication and fellowship. Love is the foundation of a successful family.

LOVE IS THE FOUNDATION OF THE NATION

Love for one's country is the foundation of a nation. Without this kind of love to bind people together, everyone becomes a law unto himself, and the result is anarchy. Where there is a lack of love there is also the destruction of the individual spirit. Love has to be the cohesive element of society. It is the basic ingredient in any mixing bowl.

National honor is national property of the highest
value.

JAMES MONROE

Unfortunately, the shortages of consumer products we are
now experiencing demonstrate to us that the idea of national
love and goodwill is not always a reality. Competition for a
full tank of gas or a loaf of bread when it is in short supply often
peels back an individual's thin veneer of love and concern for
others and leaves the real emotions of the heart showing. In
times of stress, our true colors unfurl for all to see.

LOVE IS THE NEED OF ALL PEOPLE

Some years ago, New York City had a murder mystery which
was finally solved by the arrest of several notorious criminals,
among them a man named Jack Rose. After the case was
settled and the convicted criminals imprisoned, Jack Rose said
something like this: "I always believed that there must be a
God somewhere. But when I gave Him thought, I felt He was
so far away, and so occupied with great things, that He knew
nothing about me. I am sure I never would have become a
criminal if the thought had ever entered my mind that God
cared anything about me."

Love is the reason for God's concern about man's salvation.
The apostle John writes, "For God so loved the world, that he
gave his only begotten Son" (John 3:16). God gave because
He loved. God's love for us makes us worth something. It
gives us a sense of purpose, a reason for living. Life without
God's love is absolute despair. And yet millions of people in
this world have never even heard the story of God's love.

> Do you know the world is dying
> For a little bit of love?
> Everywhere we hear them sighing,
> For a little bit of love.
>
> ANONYMOUS

A young Negro Puerto Rican grew up in New York City, at war within himself. He never knew where he belonged; he trusted no one, and his days and nights were filled with hatred and rebellion. From gang fighting he turned to narcotics. Heroin became his god, and because he had learned the power of fear early, he became a stick-up artist. It was routine for him to hold a knife against someone's throat in order to get money for drugs.

Then one day he stumbled into a little mission church. It was not beautiful to look at; it had cracks in the walls, but love flowed out from the people to soften his tough heart in a way he had never known before. Through the clean bed the superintendent offered him, the food, the conversations with other addicts, the services which revealed Jesus Christ, and the work assignments, God's love began to heal the deep scars in his life. The love of God he now contains makes life not a hateful indignity to run from, but an opportunity to help others know the power of God's Spirit.

> There are more people who wish to be loved than there are willing to love.
>
> CHAMFORT

LOVE IS THE PROOF OF SALVATION

Love is also the proof of genuine salvation. John declares, "We know that we have passed from death unto life, because we love the brethren. He that loveth not his brother abideth in death" (1 John 3:14). It is very plain that our love for others is a definite test of our own personal salvation. John does not say that our love for others is the cause for our salvation, but it is the indispensable proof that we are saved. If our faith does not result in love, then there is something wrong with our faith. "Pure religion and undefiled before God and the Father is this: To visit the fatherless and widows in their affliction, and to keep himself unspotted from the world" (James 1:27).

The young Puerto Rican boy whose life was transformed was a product of saving love. It was God's love that changed him, but it was a love that was channeled through real people. Their interest in that boy was more than just human concern. It was God's love—agape love in action. And it was a genuine demonstration of their faith in Jesus Christ.

The Lord Jesus Christ Himself made love the mark of Christianity when He said, "By this shall all men know that ye are my disciples, if ye have love one to another" (John 13:35). Throughout His earthly ministry our Lord repeatedly commanded His followers to love one another. "A new commandment I give unto you," Jesus told His disciples, "That you love one another; as I have loved you" (John 13:34). Jesus is our supreme example. He is the author of love.

Many people seem to think that they can simply ignore this command of Christ. But Christ's words are so basic to the Christian life that failure on our part to heed this admonition can render us totally useless in our Christian walk. Without the love of God shining through us, we cannot rightly represent God to men, nor can we ourselves be in a proper relationship with Him. This was the motivation of Paul when he declared, "The love of Christ constraineth us" (2 Corinthians 5:14). It was this same apostle Paul who declared that though he might have all gifts and all faith, without love he would have nothing. (See 1 Corinthians 13:1-5.)

> Real love is the universal language—understood by all. You may have every accomplishment or give your body to be burned; but, if love is lacking, all this will profit you and the cause of Christ nothing.
>
> HENRY DRUMMOND

God's love is not cheap or sentimental. It is priceless and incomparable! The way of love is God's way, and His way is the only way to abundant and victorious living. It is the best way. Life apart from God's love is failure. In fact, living without loving is merely existing!

The prize of love can be gained only when we are willing to pay the price. It may involve heartbreak, suffering, disappointment, frustration, exhaustion, and tears. The call to love is not for the halfhearted. It is a full-time, lifelong vocation. Though it is not an easy road, it is a satisfying one. Those who embark on it would never turn back for any simple pleasures of the old turned-in way of life. It is the exciting peak that must be climbed, the zenith of all Christian experience. Love is the greatest!

> God is the source of love.
> Christ is the proof of love.
> Service is the expression of love.
> Boldness is the outcome of love.

The great prime minister of England, William Gladstone, knew something of the fulfillment a life of love can bring. While facing one of the great crises of his political life, he sat writing one morning at two o'clock the speech with which he hoped to win a great political victory in the House of Commons the next day. At that hour there came to his door the mother of a poor, dying cripple, asking him to come and bring some message of hope and cheer to her hopeless boy. Without hesitation the great Commoner left the preparation of his speech, and spent the night leading the child to Christ. Staying till the early dawn, he closed the eyes of the dead child and went back to his home and faced his day with a smile of confidence, peace, and power.

Later that morning Gladstone said to a friend, "I am the happiest man in the world today." He had been able to demonstrate the love of Christ to a poor little child in a tenement house, in the name of the Master. A few hours later he made the greatest speech of his life in the House of Commons carrying his cause to a triumphant success. William Gladstone knew the motivation of Christ's love!

Do you have the love of Christ in your life? Have you made

His love the foundation of all that you are? Has God's love become your supreme goal? By God's grace determine to know the fulness of God's love in your life from this day foward.

SUGGESTED PRAYER

I thank Thee for Thy great love. In Thy love I find purpose for living. In Thy love I find assurance of salvation. In Thy love I find everlasting safety. I pray, with the apostle Paul, that God's love would abound in me so that others will be aware of Jesus Christ. Amen.

REMINDERS

- "A new commandment I give unto you, That ye love one another" (John 13:34)

- God's love is not cheap or sentimental. It is priceless and incomparable!

- Living without loving is merely existing!

- The call to love is not for the halfhearted. It is a full-time, life-long vocation.

- The prize of love can be gained only when we are willing to pay the price.

1 CORINTHIANS 13

Even though I speak in human and angelic language and have no love, I am as noisy brass or a clashing cymbal. [2]And although I have the prophetic gift and see through every secret and through all that may be known, and have sufficient faith for the removal of mountains, but I have no love, I am nothing. [3]And though I give all my belongings to feed the hungry and surrender my body to be burned, but I have no love, I am not in the least benefited.

[4]Love endures long and is kind; love is not jealous; love is not out for display; [5]it is not conceited or unmannerly; it is neither self-seeking nor irritable, nor does it take account of a wrong that is suffered. [6]It takes no pleasure in injustice but sides happily with truth. [7]It bears everything in silence, has unquenchable faith, hopes under all circumstances, endures without limit.

[8]Love never fails. As for prophesyings, they will pass away; as for tongues, they will cease; as for knowledge, it will lose its meaning. [9]For our knowledge is fragmentary and so is our prophesying. [10]But when the perfect is come then the fragmentary will come to an end.

[11]When I was a child I talked like a child, thought like a child, I reasoned like a child, but on becoming a man I was through with childish ways. [12]For now we see indistinctly in a mirror, but then face to face. Now we know partly, but then we shall understand as completely as we are understood.

[13]There remain then, faith, hope, love, these three; but the greatest of these is love.

The Holy Bible: The New Berkeley Version in Modern English, ed. Gerrit Verkuyl (Grand Rapids: Zondervan, 1969). Copyright © 1945, 59, 69 by Zondervan Publishing House and used by permissoin

10

LOVE LOST AND FOUND

"I have somewhat against thee, because thou hast left thy first love" (Revelation 2:4).

Edmund Burke, in one of his speeches on English politics, mentions the decline of character in a civil statesman. He says, "The instances are exceedingly rare of men immediately passing over a clear marked line from virtue into declared vice and corruption. There are middle tints and shades between the two extremes; there is something uncertain on the confines of the two empires which they must pass through, and which renders the change easy and imperceptible."

This is often true in the spiritual realm. Samson exposed himself to evil until a moral paralysis made him oblivious to God's absence. "And he knew not that the Lord was departed from him" (Judges 16:20). The early days of King Saul were like a magnificent sunrise, only gradually did the clouds appear until blackness triumphed and he crawled off to consult the witch of Endor.

The Ephesian believers were rebuked because they left their first love. Once these Christians were industrious, God-fearing, truth-abiding people, but they lost their original drive and devotion to the Lord. "I have somewhat against thee, because thou hast left thy first love" (Revelation 2:4). History reveals that this process continued until the Ephesian church died.

WHAT IS FIRST LOVE?

What is first love? It is the love we came to know when we

were converted. It is that exciting flood of response that we experienced when God plainly assured us, "As far as the east is from the west, so far hath he removed our transgressions from us" (Psalm 103:12).

> This "first love" seeks not people, but a Person, the One who alone merits our *first* love. The "first love" is the intimate personal relationship of love which one has with our Lord Jesus Christ.
>
>   M. BASILEA SCHLINK

First love is felt with the total trust and the warm affection of the newborn soul. First love looks at the grand possibilities, not the weight of the problems. To cross each river is a stirring challenge; to climb each mountain is an adventure. Stumbling stones become stepping stones. Every obstacle is a fresh way to prove the omnipotence of God. First love is warm, radiant, and real. With wide-open arms, first love welcomes the world to its heart. It wears working clothes in the market place; it gets in gear with real people who have deep needs. First love is clean, expectant, strong, involved, and victorious.

The apostle Paul knew this kind of love firsthand. Besides possessing a brilliant mind, he was endowed with a loving heart. His soul was a furnace of concern for his generation. Writing to the people of Rome, he said, "I am debtor both to the Greeks and to the barbarians; both to the wise and to the unwise" (Romans 1:14). To the Thessalonian church he wrote, "For ye remember, brethren, our labour and travail; for laboring night and day, because we would not be chargeable unto any of you, we preached unto you the gospel of God" (1 Thessalonians 2:9).

> No one can live without being a debtor; no one should live without being a creditor.
>
>   N. J. PANIN

The word travail indicates a deep concern, a struggle, even pain. Day and night Paul labored so that he would not be indebtcd to his generation. I can hear him say, "I have a debt, I have an obligation, I must share the gospel." To experience real salvation is to love people. Personal salvation and loving people are synonymous. To remain self-centered and silent in the light of salvation is to become some sort of monster.

One of the faces of love is a willingness to be involved in another person's pain. And you might as well know right away that this will mean that you are going to suffer, too, along with the one who is troubled. Loving is not easy and not free of hurt.

We human beings are constructed in a very complex way. It is our natural tendency to avoid pain. We do not like to feel uncomfortable. We are masters at building protective devices into our lives. When we are rejected by another person, we almost unconsciously figure out how we can avoid that kind of hurt again.

When someone screams at us or spits out some spiteful comment, our natural reaction is to protect our own self-image by talking back or screaming louder. We are exceedingly clever at defending ourselves from hurt, from pain, from discomfort. Only as we keep pouring the love of God into the big, demanding hole of self, are we prepared to take on the pain, the travail that Paul talked about.

> God does not comfort us that we may be comfortable but that we may be comforters.
>
> ALEXANDER NOWELL

The intensity of Paul's involvement is seen in depth of his words to the church at Rome. "I have great heaviness and continual sorrow in my heart. For I could wish that myself were accursed from Christ for my brethren, my kinsmen according to the flesh" (Romans 9:2-3). This is redemptive love. In plain talk, Paul is saying, "I am prepared to go to hell, if by so doing my friends and countrymen will share in the gospel."

Isn't this staggering? This kind of love is difficult to comprehend.

This same spirit was shared by Moses when he interceded
for Israel. Moses prayed, "Oh, this people have sinned a great
sin, and have made them gods of gold. Yet now, if thou wilt
forgive their sin—; and if not, blot me, I pray thee, out of thy
book which thou hast written" (EXODUS 32:31-32). Oh, what
love! What identification! Both Moses and Paul were motivated by supernatural love.

The Ephesian believers were hard-working, patient, preserv-
ing, and thoroughly orthodox. The apostle John commended
them for many virtues. The Christ of the candlesticks is not
blind to the beauties of His people. He loves us, and He gave
His life for us. He desires to see our light burning brightly.
However, in spite of the outstanding virtues of the Ephesian
church, the Lord of the lampstands could tell when their love
declined into a noisy Pharisaic busyness. With the pain of a
neglected love, He calls, "I have somewhat against thee"
(Revelation 2:4).

How Is First Love Lost?

How is this love lost? First love is lost because of sin, according to Matthew 24:12. "Because iniquity shall abound,
the love of many shall grow cold." Centuries ago Isaiah said,
"Your iniquities have separated between you and your God,
and your sins have hid his face from you, that he will not hear"
(Isaiah 59:2).

Sin dulls first love. It is a wall of separation that builds up
between man and God. Sin darkens the light of our life. It
blurs our understanding of the mind of God. Sin sears our
spiritual conscience and drains our spiritual power.

> A seared conscience is one whose warning voice has
> been suppressed and perverted habitually, so that

eventually instead of serving as a guide, it only confirms the person in his premeditatedly evil course.

ROBERT J. LITTLE

I heard a story once of an American eagle that was observed soaring magnificently into the sky. Shortly it faltered, stopped, and plunged toward the earth, dead. When the eagle was examined, it was discovered that a small weasel had dug its claws into the abdomen of the bird, risen with the eagle into the sky, and drained the life-blood while the eagle tried to escape. Sin is like that. It robs us of power and life itself. If we take a friendly attitude toward sin, then Christ must take harsh measures with us.

Jesus sets before us a bold, unvarnished question: Are you a bride or a whore? The two possibilities are related: it is only possible to become a whore because God has called us to be a bride. The call to love God creates the alternative, that we squander our love faithlessly. Jesus looks to us for the love of a bride. Any other love which possesses our heart brings us into the state of spiritual adultery.

M. BASILEA SCHLINK

Sin is the obstacle to first love. It appears in two main forms—open rebellion against God, and a neglect of obedience to the revealed will of God. One of the prevailing problems of the church today is the obsession to be accepted. We get too concerned about what people will think. Sophistication has all but smothered first love. The church is on an intellectual binge to the point of cancelling the effect of the cross.

Sophistication is the spirit's foe.

GEORGE SANTAYANA

Sometimes we Christians are so tactful that we don't make contact at all. Paul, with all of his brilliance, would not permit the wisdom of this world to cancel out the power of the gospel. "For the preaching of the cross is to them that perish foolishness; but unto us who are saved it is the power of God" (1 Corinthians 1:18). All sin has a chilling effect on first love.

Another way we lose the love we first knew is by trying to enshrine it and preserve it, by failing to let it bubble up through all of our living experience.

Perhaps the clearest way to describe this failing of love is to draw a parallel within the stage of human marriage. The first tremendously overwhelming stage is what we have come to call falling in love. It is so urgent, so total that we stand alone with our beloved as though there were no one else in all the world. We want to retain the flame, the intensity, the one-and-only feeling forever. So we marry—for keeps. But soon we begin to discover that the world is still with us after all. We are not two people alone in a miraculous vacuum of love. We are a bit surprised to learn that we still have parents and in-laws, brothers and sisters, business associates and neighbors, old friends and strangers at the door. And somehow we have to begin to make room for all of these presences in our new life together.

It takes time. It takes arguments and tears. These persons make demands on our marriage relationship which we don't particularly want. But we either learn how to keep our love warm and alive, while accommodating other people, or we get drawn into the complex process and pulled away from our loved one.

People, appointments, work, and a thousand other things, begin to pry us apart, and before we know it, the separation is almost unbridgeable. We look back across the gulf and say, "She's not the same person I married. We have so little in common. We really aren't compatible at all."

Is it possible that we as Christians fail in this same way as we begin to get involved in service? As we begin to stand back and look at this revolutionary love that has demanded total commitment of us, what do we see? Do we get so preoccupied with going to meetings, sounding well when we pray out loud, working on church committees or organizations, meeting the local standards of church behavior, watching our own piety become noticeable to others, that we lose sight of—don't have time for—the great Lover who first won us?

> I came to see that my relationship to my Lord Jesus Christ, with the passing years, had eroded away something like a marriage gone humdrum. What did I do when I found a little pocket of spare time, on a Sunday, or a holiday? I couldn't wait to get together with other people—people I liked, people with whom I had something in common—so we could share ideas and experiences. Or I read a stimulating book. Or I went out to enjoy nature. I even plunged further into my work, doing things that I normally didn't have time for. But to go to Jesus—to give Him first claim on even my spare time—that I did not do.
>
> M. BASILEA SCHLINK

What happens as *you* begin to integrate this new love into your home life, your marriage, your office routine, your shop conversations, your school work? Do you stay in tune with the wondrous love that won you, and let the Holy Spirit show you how to share this freshness with others? Or do you hug it to yourself for fear of losing it, for fear of failing? Do you get so busy with your chores, your deadlines, your concern with what others think, that you lose touch with the Holy Spirit and wonder if the experience was ever real in the first place?

HOW IS FIRST LOVE RESTORED?

The big, and very practical, question is, How is first love restored? The first step is to remember. The Lord is always found exactly where you left Him. He calls out, "Remember . . . from where thou art fallen" (Revelation 2:5). Remember when you enjoyed the presence of God in everyday living? Can you recall the moments of satisfying communion in prayer? Remember the pure happy relationship to Jesus Christ you once enjoyed? Remember when the hymns of the church sang often in your mind through the day's work? Remember when you wept, unashamedly and joyously, out of gratitude to Jesus for His goodness upon your life? Remember when you sought out loved ones and friends to tell them what Jesus was doing for you? "Remember from where thou art fallen."

> Let us be glad and rejoice, and give honour to him: for the marriage of the Lamb is come, and his wife hath made herself ready. And to her was granted that she should be arrayed in fine linen, clean and white; for the fine linen is the righteousness of the saints (Revelation 19:7-8).

The second step is to repent. Holy memories should lead to holy action. The message of repentance has been nearly forgotten in our day. To repent means to turn around. It involves a change of mind, attitude, and conduct. It means to go back simply and humbly and start all over. David, the man after God's own heart, enjoyed thrilling companionship with God. Yet during many careless periods of life, he went his own way. He saw a woman he wanted, he saw leadership he wanted, he saw power and status, and he connived to get what he wanted. The flesh asserted itself in all its ugliness. God said no, but David said yes, and he sinned greatly.

The Scriptures ask, "Can two walk together, except they be agreed?" (Amos 3:3). The answer is emphatically, *no*. When David walked after his own desires, he walked without God. Many people think they walk with God when actually they have walked off and left Him, because they are living contrary to God's Word. In David's life, the glad day of repentance always dawned and David would cry, "Against thee, thee only, have I sinned, and done this evil in thy sight" (Psalm 51:4). Each time David confessed his sin, immediately fellowship was restored, and God and David walked together once more.

Man is born with his back toward God. When he truly repents, he turns right around and faces God.

D. L. MOODY

To confess means to say what God has said; to agree with God. David had said, "Lord, I'm wrong, and Thou art right." This is confession.

The third step is to return. This changed attitude results in a return in conduct to what John calls first works. This is the result of repentance.

What does John mean by first works? Surely this means daily fellowship with God. First works also means to serve others in a spontaneous sharing of the things of God, to be mastered by the needs about us. First works are not stingy but generous. The redemptive Word which we take in our daily fellowship with God issues forth in a redemptive work to others. The world outside the church is weary of listening to us talk without feeling the concrete manifestations of our love. God's Holy Spirit can empower us to live and act as loudly as we talk: first works is the twin of first love. Positive action in moving out of our own preoccupations to care for other people demonstrates our love for Jesus Christ. If this seems so very difficult, try praying specifically for someone you want to care about. Prayer often leads to love.

The apostle John concludes with a severe warning, "I will come unto thee quickly, and will remove thy lampstand out of its place, except thou repent" (Revelation 2:5). For the church of Ephesus it was either revival or removal. Nevertheless, the Ephesians refused the message of John, and they suffered the consequences—they were removed!

I have personally witnessed Christians who have been removed by God because they refused to heed His rebuke, as were Ananias and Sapphira when they persisted in living a lie. To the Corinthians, who shared in the ordinance of the Lord's table carelessly, Paul wrote, "For this cause many are weak and sickly among you, and many sleep" (1 Corinthians 11:30). Obviously some of these were removed because they refused to change their careless ways.

Where is Ephesus today? Where is the light that once burned there intensely? The light is long gone, and the church of Ephesus exists no more.

God's message to us today is the same as it was to these believers of the first century—remember, repent, and return! "Beloved," says Jude, "keep yourselves in the love of God" (vv. 20-21). What more can we ask today?

SUGGESTED PRAYER

Lord, help me to be quick to repent of all my sin. Help me once again to do first works in the flaming spirit of first love. May the light of my life burn brightly in this dark age. Amen.

REMINDERS

- "I have somewhat against thee, because thou hast left thy first love" (Revelation 2:4).
- First love looks at the grand possibilities, not the weight of the problems.
- First love is warm, radiant, and real.
- "No one can live without being a debtor; no one should live without being a creditor." N. J. PANIN
- Sin dulls first love.
- The Lord is always found exactly where you left Him.
- For the church of Ephesus it was either revival or removal.
- God's message to us today is . . . remember, repent, and return!
- "Beloved . . . keep yourselves in the love of God" (Jude 20-21).

APPENDIX

SELECTED SCRIPTURE PORTIONS ON LOVE

And thou shalt love the LORD thy God with all thine heart, and with all thy soul, and with all thy might (DEUTERONOMY 6:5).

The LORD did not set his love upon you, nor choose you, because ye were more in number than any people; for ye were the fewest of all people. But because the LORD loved you, and because he would keep the oath which he had sworn unto your fathers, hath the LORD brought you out with a mighty hand, and redeemed you out of the house of bondage, from the hand of Pharaoh king of Egypt (DEUTERONOMY 7:7-8).

Oh, love the LORD, all ye his saints; for the LORD preserveth the faithful, and plentifully rewardeth the proud doer (PSALM 31:23).

A friend loveth at all times, and a brother is born for adversity (PROVERBS 17:17).

Set me as a seal upon thine heart, as a seal upon thine arm, for love is strong as death, jealousy is cruel as sheol; its coals are coals of fire, which hath a most vehement flame. Many waters cannot quench love, neither can the floods drown it. If a man would give all the substance of his house for love, he would utterly be rejected (SONG OF SOLOMON 8:6-7).

The LORD hath appeared of old unto me, saying, Yea, I have loved thee with an everlasting love; therefore, with loving-kindness have I drawn thee (JEREMIAH 31:3).

Ye have heard that it hath been said, Thou shalt love thy neighbor, and hate thine enemy; But I say unto you, Love your enemies, bless them that curse you, do good to them that hate you, and pray for them who despitefully use you, and persecute you; That ye may be the sons of your Father, who is in heaven; for he maketh his sun to

137

rise on the evil and on the good, and sendeth rain on the just and on the unjust. For if ye love them who love you, what reward have ye? Do not even the tax collectors the same? And if ye greet your brethren only, what do ye more than others? Do not even the heathen so? Be ye, therefore, perfect, even as your Father, who is in heaven, is perfect (MATTHEW 5:43-48).

Jesus said unto him, Thou shalt love the Lord thy God with all thy heart, and with all thy soul, and with all thy mind. This is the first and great commandment. And the second is like it, Thou shalt love thy neighbor as thyself. On these two commandments hang all the law and the prophets (MATTHEW 22:37-40).

But I say unto you that hear, Love your enemies, do good to them who hate you, Bless them that curse you, and pray for them who despitefully use you (LUKE 6:27-28).

Wherefore I say unto thee, Her sins, which are many, are forgiven; for she loved much: but to whom little is forgiven, the same loveth little (LUKE 7:47).

And, behold, a certain lawyer stood up, and tested him, saying, Master, what shall I do to inherit eternal life? He said unto him, What is written in the law? How readest thou? And he, answering, said, Thou shalt love the Lord thy God with all thy heart, and with all thy soul, and with all thy strength, and with all thy mind; and thy neighbor as thyself. And he said unto him, Thou hast answered right: this do, and thou shalt live. But he, desiring to justify himself, said unto Jesus, And who is my neighbor? And Jesus, answering, said, A certain man went down from Jerusalem to Jericho, and fell among thieves, who stripped him of his raiment, and wounded him, and departed, leaving him half dead. And by chance there came down a certain priest that way: and when he saw him, he passed by on the other side. And likewise a Levite, when he was at the place, came and looked on him, and passed by on the other side. But a certain Samaritan, as he journeyed, came where he was; and when he saw him, he had compassion on him, And went to him, and bound up his wounds, pouring in oil and wine, and set him on his own beast, and brought him to an inn, and took care of him. And on the next day, when he departed, he took out two denarii, and gave them to the host, and said unto him, Take care of him; and whatever thou spendest more, when I come again, I will repay thee. Which, now, of these three, thinkest thou, was neighbor unto him that fell among the thieves? And he said, He that showed mercy on him. Then said Jesus unto him, Go, and do thou likewise (Luke 10:25-37).

If ye love me, keep my commandments. And I will pray the Father, and he shall give you another Comforter, that he may abide with you forever. . . . He that hath my commandments, and keepeth them, he it is that loveth me; and he that loveth me shall be loved of my Father, and I will love him, and will manifest myself to him (John 14:15-16, 21).

As the Father hath loved me, so have I loved you; continue ye in my love. If ye keep my commandments, ye shall abide in my love, even as I have kept my Father's commandments, and abide in his love. These things have I spoken unto you, that my joy might remain in you, and that your joy might be full. This is my commandment, that ye love one another, as I have loved you. Greater love hath no man than this, that a man lay down his life for his friends. Ye are my friends, if ye do whatever I command you (John 15:9-14).

So when they had dined, Jesus saith to Simon Peter, Simon, son of Jonah, lovest thou me more than these? He saith unto him, Yea, Lord; thou knowest that I love thee. He saith unto him, Feed my lambs. He saith to him again the second time, Simon, son of Jonah, lovest thou me? He saith unto him, Yea, Lord; thou knowest that I love thee. He saith unto him, Feed my sheep (John 21:15-16).

And hope maketh not ashamed, because the love of God is shed abroad in our hearts by the Holy Spirit who is given unto us (Romans 5:5).

But God commendeth his love toward us, in that, while we were yet sinners, Christ died for us (Romans 5:8).

And we know that all things work together for good to them that love God, to them who are the called according to his purpose. . . . What shall separate us from the love of Christ? Shall tribulation, or distress, or persecution, or famine, or nakedness, or peril, or sword? As it is written, For thy sake we are killed all the day long; we are accounted as sheep for the slaughter. Nay, in all these things we are more than conquerors through him that loved us. For I am persuaded that neither death, nor life, nor angels, nor principalities, nor powers, nor things present, nor things to come, Nor height, nor depth, nor any other creation, shall be able to separate us from the love of God, which is in Christ Jesus, our Lord (ROMANS 8:28, 35-39).

Let love be without hypocrisy. Abhor that which is evil; cling to that which is good. Be kindly affectioned one to another with brotherly love, in honor preferring one another (ROMANS 12:9-10).

Owe no man any thing, but to love one another; for he that loveth another hath fulfilled the law. For this, Thou shalt not commit adultery, Thou shalt not kill, Thou shalt not steal, Thou shalt not bear false witness, Thou shalt not covet; and if there be any other commandment, it is briefly comprehended in this saying, namely, Thou shalt love thy neighbor as thyself. Love worketh no ill to its neighbors; therefore, love is the fulfilling of the law (ROMANS 13:8-10).

Now as touching things offered unto idols, we know that we all have knowledge. Knowledge puffeth up, but love edifieth. And if any man think that he knoweth anything, he knoweth nothing yet as he ought to know. But if any man love God, the same is known of him (1 CORINTHIANS 8:1-3).

But if any have caused grief, he hath not grieved me, but in part: that I may not burden you all. Sufficient to such a man is this punishment, which was inflicted by the many. So that on the contrary ye ought rather to forgive him, and comfort him, lest perhaps such a one should be swallowed up with overmuch sorrow. Wherefore, I beseech you that ye would confirm your love toward him (2 CORINTHIANS 2:5-8).

Behold, the third time I am ready to come to you; and I will not be burdensome to you, for I seek not yours, but you. For the children ought not to lay up for the parents, but the parents for the children.

And I will very gladly spend and be spent for you; though the more abundantly I love you, the less I be loved (2 CORINTHIANS 12:14-15).

But the fruit of the Spirit is love, joy, peace, long-suffering, gentleness, goodness, faith, Meekness, self-control; against such there is no law (GALATIANS 5:22-23).

Having predestinated us unto the adoption of sons by Jesus Christ to himself, according to the good pleasure of his will, To the praise of the glory of his grace, through which he hath made us accepted in the Beloved; In whom we have redemption through his blood, the forgiveness of sins, according to the riches of his grace (EPHESIANS 1:5-7).

But God, who is rich in mercy, for his great love with which he loved us, Even when we were dead in sins, hath made us alive together with Christ (by grace ye are saved), And hath raised us up together, and made us sit together in heavenly places in Christ Jesus. . . . Not of works, lest any man should boast (EPHESIANS 2:4-6, 9).

That Christ may dwell in your hearts by faith; that ye, being rooted and grounded in love, May be able to comprehend, with all saints, what is the breadth, and length, and depth, and height, And to know the love of Christ, which passeth knowledge, that ye might be filled with all the fullness of God (EPHESIANS 3:17-19).

With all lowliness and meekness, with long-suffering, forbearing one another in love (EPHESIANS 4:2).

That we henceforth be no more children, tossed to and fro, and carried about with every wind of doctrine, by the sleight of men, and cunning craftiness, by which they lie in wait to deceive; But. speaking the truth in love, may grow up into him in all things, who is the head, even Christ (EPHESIANS 4:14-15).

And this I pray, that your love may abound yet more and more in knowledge and in all judgment (PHILIPPIANS 1:9).

That their hearts might be comforted, being knit together in love and unto all riches of the full assurance of understanding, to the acknowledgement of the mystery of God, and of the Father, and of Christ (COLOSSIANS 2:2).

Wives, submit yourselves unto your own husbands, as it is fit in the Lord. Husbands, love your wives, and be not bitter against them. Children, obey your parents in all things; for this is well-pleasing unto the Lord (COLOSSIANS 3:18-20).

So, being affectionately desirous of you, we were willing to have imparted unto you, not the gospel of God only but also our own souls, because ye were dear unto us (1 THESSALONIANS 2:8).

But, as touching brotherly love, ye need not that I write unto you; for ye yourselves are taught of God to love one another. And, indeed, ye do it toward all the brethren who are in all Macedonia. But we beseech you, brethren, that ye increase more and more, And that ye study to be quiet, and to do your own business, and to work with your own hands, as we commanded you (1 THESSALONIANS 4:9-11).

But we are bound to give thanks always to God for you, brethren beloved of the Lord, because God hath from the beginning chosen you to salvation through sanctification of the Spirit and belief of the truth (2 THESSALONIANS 2:13).

Now the end of the commandment is love out of a pure heart, and of a good conscience, and of faith unfeigned (1 TIMOTHY 1:5).

And the grace of our Lord was exceedingly abundant with faith and love which is in Christ Jesus (1 TIMOTHY 1:14).

For God hath not given us the spirit of fear, but of power, and of love, and of a sound mind (2 TIMOTHY 1:7).

Flee also youthful lusts, but follow righteousness, faith, love, peace, with them that call on the Lord out of a pure heart (2 TIMOTHY 2:22).

Let brotherly love continue. Be not forgetful to entertain strangers; for thereby some have entertained angels unawares (HEBREWS 13:1-2).

Seeing that ye have purified your souls in obeying the truth through the Spirit unto unfeigned love of the brethren, see that ye love one another with a pure heart fervently (1 PETER 1:22).

Finally, be ye all of one mind, having compassion one of another, love as brethren, be pitiful, be courteous, Not rendering evil for evil, or railing for railing, but on the contrary, blessing, knowing that ye are called to this, that ye should inherit a blessing (1 PETER 3:8-9).

And above all things have fervent love among yourselves; for love shall cover the multitude of sins. Use hospitality one to another without grudging. As every man hath received the gift, even so minister the same one to another, as good stewards of the manifold grace of God (1 PETER 4:8-10).

Simon Peter, a servant and an apostle of Jesus Christ, to them that have obtained like precious faith with us through the righteousness of God and our Savior, Jesus Christ: Grace and peace be multiplied unto you through the knowledge of God, and of Jesus, our Lord, According as his divine power hath given unto us all things that pertain unto life and godliness, through the knowledge of him that hath called us to glory and virtue; By which are given unto us exceedingly great and precious promises, that by these ye might be partakers of the divine nature, having escaped the corruption that is in the world through lust. And beside this, giving all diligence, add to your faith virtue; and to virtue, knowledge; And to knowledge, self control; and to self-control, patience; and to patience, godliness; And to godliness, brotherly kindness; and to brotherly kindness, love (2 PETER 1:1-7).

And by this we do know that we know him, if we keep his commandments. He that saith, I know him, and keepeth not his commandments, is a liar, and the truth is not in him. But whosoever keepeth his word, in him verily is the love of God perfected; by this know we that we are in him. He that saith he abideth in him ought himself also so to walk, even as he walked (1 JOHN 2:3-6).

We know that we have passed from death unto life, because we love the brethren. He that loveth not his brother abideth in death.

Whosoever hateth his brother is a murderer; and ye know that no murderer hath eternal life abiding in him. By this perceive we the love of God, because he laid down his life for us; and we ought to lay down our lives for the brethren. But whosoever hath this world's good, and seeth his brother have need, and shutteth up his compassions from him, how dwelleth the love of God in him? My little children, let us not love in word, neither in tongue, but in deed and in truth (1 JOHN 3:14-18).

Beloved, if God so loved us, we ought also to love one another. No man hath seen God at any time. If we love one another, God dwelleth in us, and his love is perfected in us. . . . There is no fear in love, but perfect love casteth out fear, because fear hath punishment (1 JOHN 4:11-12, 18).

Keep yourselves in the love of God, looking for the mercy of our Lord Jesus Christ unto eternal life (JUDE 21).

Unto the angel of the church of Ephesus write: These things saith he that holdeth the seven stars in his right hand, who walketh in the midst of the seven golden lampstands. I know thy works, and thy labor, and thy patience, and how thou canst not bear them who are evil; and thou hast tried them who say they are apostles, and are not, and hast found them liars; And hast borne, and hast patience, and for my name's sake hast labored, and hast not fainted. Nevertheless, I have somewhat against thee, because thou hast left thy first love. Remember, therefore, from where thou art fallen, and repent, and do the first works, or else I will come unto thee quickly, and will remove thy lampstand out of its place, except thou repent (REVELATION 2:1-5).